THE ORGANIC ENTREPRENEUR

Also by the author

The Naked Millionaire

THE ORGANIC ENTREPRENEUR

Cultivating the Conscious Capitalist

Maxine Hyndman

INSOMNIAC PRESS

Library and Archives Canada Cataloguing in Publication

Hyndman, Maxine C. 1965-

The organic entrepreneur : cultivating the conscious capitalist / Maxine Hyndman.

Contains index.

ISBN 1-897178-28-X
    1. Business ethics. I. Title.
HF5387.H96 2006   174'.4   C2006-903484-2

The publisher gratefully acknowledges the support of the Canada Council, the Ontario Arts Council and the Department of Canadian Heritage through the Book Publishing Industry Development Program.

Printed and bound in Canada

Insomniac Press
192 Spadina Avenue, Suite 403
Toronto, Ontario, Canada, M5T 2C2
www.insomniacpress.com

Dedication

To three of the strongest women I know who have helped me define and build whealth:

To my mother, Gloria, who planted the seed of entrepreneurship in me from the time I was a child with her relentless pursuit of freedom through doing what you love;

To my daughter, Dalma, who gave me the reason to keep pursuing the means with which to support both her and myself, on my own terms; and

To my sister-in-law, Shelley, without whose brilliant guidance, vision, and steadfast support neither this book nor the first would ever have seen the light of day!

There is no agony like having an untold story inside you.
—Zora Neale Hurston

There is one thing in this world which must never be forgotten. Human beings come into this world to do a particular work. If you forget everything else, and not this, there's nothing to worry about. If you remember everything else and forget your true work, then you will have done nothing in your life.
—Rumi

Remy
(604) 506-9231

Table of Contents

Introduction   11

Winter   19

Winter's Incubation   21

The Creative Process in Winter   22

Greater Purpose – The Soul of Your Business   25

Values – The Heart of Your Business   30

Secrets and Surprises   33

Dreaming Your Business Awake   39

Goals to Grow By   43

Patience   45

Important Observations in Winter   48

Creating the Structure – A Business Map   49

Financials   55

Exit Strategy   55

Personal Environments – An Introduction   56

Business and the Alchemy of Self   64

Listening 101   67

Comfort Zones   70

God and the Devil Live Here   72

Reflecting on the Season   73

Spring   75

Spring's Creation   77

Rebirth   78

Creativity in Spring   79

Action   80

Actions, Emotions, Procrastination, and the Big Picture   82

Designing Your Business   87

Respect   88

Money and Meaning   89

Money and Creativity   91

Money and Fear   93

Money and Power   96

Principles of Organic Marketing   96

The Benefits of Basic Needs 108
Southern Exposure 111
Why the Shame in Marketing? 112
Owning Your Craft 114
If Wishes Were Horses 115
When Opportunity Knocks, 117
    Do I Have to Answer?
Sun Worship 119

Summer 121
Summer's Abundance 123
Abundance 124
Creativity 127
Communication 130
Consciousness 135
Momentum 139
Connecting and Collaborating 143
Help Is *Virtually* Around the Corner 145
How to Collaborate in Business with Anyone 147
Winning – The Highs and Lows 152
Control 153
Grounded in Gratitude 155
Giving 158

Autumn 163
Autumn's Economy 165
Personal Environments 167
Conscious Economics 171
Beliefs – Our Dirty Little Secret 173
Your Health 176
Compassion 178
Discipline 180
Service 181
Freedom 183

Afterword 185
Index 189

Introduction

Discontent and disorder were signs of energy and hope, not of despair.
—Dame Veronica Wedgwood, OM

Access The Power

It was Italy. I was in love. It was divine and *I* was discontented.

What exactly is discontentment? It is the restless longing for better circumstances—and I was definitely restless. Almost all entrepreneurs are at times and that is actually a very good thing. Discontentment is essential to propel us from the inertia and listlessness that has gripped much of our society toward the self-expression and fulfillment our beings long for. At the time, however, I had no idea that the journey of building a business often begins in earnest with this obnoxious ingredient.

I wish with all my soul that I had understood then that my discontentment was divine. As author Sarah Ban Breathnach writes in her book, *Simple Abundance*:

> It is the grit in the oyster before the pearl. This creative second chance is when we come into our own. When we finally claim our own lives and wrestle our futures from fate. When we learn how to spin straw into gold. When we realize gratefully that we can live by our own lights if we access the Power.

That grit, that discontentment, is what is needed to drive the would-be entrepreneur out of complacency, dependency, and fear of the future into an experience of self-actualization on every level. It is not meant to be a curse or a handicap. If we use it wisely, we see it signals a perfect opportunity to fundamentally change our lives for the better. That discontentment is the pumice that smoothes out the rough edges of our lives that have accumulated over time.

So many years ago, I was without this insight as I set out to start my own fabric export company. After that, it was an Internet business, then a marketing consultancy, and later a magazine. My winter of discontentment seemed to last for over twelve years—twelve years of searching for meaning in my life through business after business, some of my own creation and other times as an employee. At the age of thirty-eight, I had created and worked for so many businesses in so many industries that I most definitely felt like I hadn't a clue what it took to be a successful entrepreneur. Year after year, business after business, I attempted to squeeze myself into business models that were foreign to my inherent nature. I would take a great idea and try to mould it into an acceptable form based on the business paradigms I saw already out there instead of building my business from what I knew I had inside.

Eventually, I learned that there is much more to business than attaining what others deem to be "success." In fact, it is of the utmost importance that you first identify and articulate to yourself what business means to *you*. As I did this, I began trying a different approach. And it worked!

Ultimately, I came to accept and respect the fact that entrepreneurship is my true state of being, but it had to be an organic process, one in keeping with my values and deepest nature. Only then was I was able to see the overall design of my entrepreneurial life, like a grand patchwork quilt made from the remnants of each business I had built and each position I had held. What's more, I began to understand my Greater Purpose, that unique way in which each person contributes to the world. Every single experience had helped in some way to build toward a distinct and comprehensive vision of the services I was to offer.

Today, I am an author, money and marketing coach, and a highly creative entrepreneur. My business life has taken zig-zag turns, gut-wrenching deviations, and some serious nose-dives—oh, yes, and it has had the odd moments of peace and contentment. But it was that way for a reason. My organic business has led me here, to this point where I am now helping others to be entrepreneurs who respect *their* inherent nature, their environment, and their values, because the ripple effect of such a shift will be businesses that respect individuals, cultures, the environment, and the basic values of humanity in general.

The entrepreneur always has been and always will be an important part of human evolution, every bit as much as big businesses. Many of us are disgusted, disillusioned, and discontented with big business, but we shouldn't be. Businesses are built by people—individuals with or without integrity, those with and without respect, and so if we wish to build better businesses, we must start by being better people, better entrepreneurs.

This book does not denounce the value of business as it currently exists, nor is it intended to deride those who choose to run traditional businesses. This book is a quest, a call, and an answer for those who are interested in finding a *healthier* way of doing business. For indeed a new type of entrepreneur has emerged from the mist of reckless ambition and endless greed. This new type of entrepreneur is motivated less by *just* the bottom line and more by honouring the need for authenticity and respecting the integrity of their community, humanity, and their souls.

These new entrepreneurs listen, they allow themselves to feel, they give generously of their money and their time, they seek balance and fulfillment. They no longer believe the lie that to be successful in business, one has to leave one's morals, values, beliefs, and soul at the door in order to enter the gilded halls of enterprise. These organic entrepreneurs, as I call them, respect the soil in which they are planted and work within the cycles of their nature and the nature of their environment to find lasting success, meaning and balance in their lives and the lives of their businesses.

This new brand of entrepreneur calls, as well, for a new business model, one that is in keeping with our natures and with the natural rhythms of life. When we think of business, we rarely think of it in terms of natural cycles, yet businesses have their own seasons through which they progress: Winter (Incubation), Spring (Creation), Summer (Abundance), Autumn (Economy). Not only that, but within the larger cycles of our businesses there are micro-cycles going on inside each business "season." As entrepreneurs, we must adapt ourselves to these cycles rather than simply viewing business as something upon which we impose our will. The organic entrepreneur learns how to do this and reaches inward to intuitively flow with ease to give and receive the abundance that comes inevitably with being a provider of employment that sustains many families, many lives, and many dreams.

I wish I had known the significance of business when I went into it in the very beginning. Business is a passion, a privilege, and a wonderful giver of financial independence, but business is not easy. Raising children is rarely easy, and having a business is a lot like raising a child from birth to, well, the end of your life: you never stop tweaking it, sharing with it, nursing it, and beaming with pride at its accomplishments. The entrepreneur knows this. There really is nothing like it!

The Organic Entrepreneur is written to share with fledgling entrepreneurs the things I wish I had known when I was just starting out. But it is also written for those in the middle part of the business journey, for those who have been disillusioned about business but who know there is more, and for those who have been banged around a bit and still want to play the game, but a much bigger game that challenges them to transform their view of community, communication, and love. We must be willing to be trans-*formed* through business before it can become the inspirational medium it has the potential to be.

This book explores the process of the organic entrepreneur, the movement through the seasons of business, from incubation to creation, abundance to economy, with wisdom and patience and love. It examines what is needed to find the rhythm that crafts a business from within your very depths, in synch with your rhythm, showing you how to thrive in your own soil.

When we plan, create, accumulate, and economize with patience, appreciation, understanding, and love, we are giving ourselves the necessary ingredients to develop better products and services that not only serve humanity but that also begin to inuitively anticipate its needs. Just as the soil holds back more nutrients during the autumn anticipating winter long before it appears, and just as summer lightning provides necessary nitrogen to the soil—a necessary plant fertilizer during the season that has the most growth—our products and services are meant to do something similar: they are meant to provide "nourishment" to humanity.

Whether your dream is to start a new bank, create a new communication tool, or bake better bread, *The Organic Entrepreneur* will help you trust your discontentment long enough for you to find the courage within yourself to ride the momentary discomfort or fear.

So let the discontentment stir you; let it flutter then beat wildly until you can no longer take its cacophony of sound and you are moved to release it in the form of a business. Then move over, get out of the way, and let it transform you—your spirit, your mind, your emotions, and, of course, your bank account!

Winter

Winter came in August full of worry, fret, and anxiety. Its long silence a yawn in my day-to-day life. How can I welcome winter's incubation when I feel it like a curse? I'm short on insight, ignorant of the fact that it is this darkness that eventually fills my purse.

Winter's Incubation

In winter, there is a hush that falls over the landscape. It is a sacred sort of silence and it's not to be avoided. For your day-to-day operations, winter might bring a dramatic decrease in phone calls or a major breakdown of office equipment that can't be fixed for a while. But don't be fooled; there is a definite pulse, though muted, which reassures you that your business is still alive, only asleep. There's no doubt about it, the silence winter brings to your business can seem suffocating and it can leave you feeling exposed and vulnerable—certainly not up to par with the "success stories" you read so much about. Get one thing straight: you made it through one more year, so be grateful your business is still alive!

When the light shines during the winter solstice, it brings a beauty unlike any other time. It's a time when the light of even the smallest success has the power to break through the gloom. We are humbled by and grateful for its luminescence. I experienced this once when my business was in a winter and I just didn't have the energy to call the media to keep the pump primed around my first book, *The Naked Millionaire*. Three calls came through that month from various sources I had called on months ago that opened the door to more opportunities to reach more people and build publicity. These rays of light lit up my whole winter and I was so grateful that it gave me the courage to look forward to a spring that would come eventually—they became moments of triumph that were lushly savoured.

When you seem to be in your deepest, darkest of nights, that is the best time to either throw a party to celebrate your continued existence or to go to one. It might seem counterintuitive, but during the winter, entrepreneurs tend to close themselves off as if being bundled in darkness were a way to avoid falling off the perceived edge. The edge exists only in our minds and even if the business doesn't make it, that simply means *one* attempt didn't bring about the desired result. Back to the drawing board. Go out and have fun even if the temptation to sit and brood is overpowering. Don't get trapped into numbness and lose sight of the wonderful things you've accomplished during the year: winning an award, hiring a great new employee, landing a review from a respected industry insider, or finishing a huge project. Look carefully at the whole picture; it's filled with riches. Resist the urge to let your mood discolour the progress you've made so far.

The Creative Process in Winter

Being an entrepreneur is a creative, personal process. Along with intuition, wisdom, perseverance, and patience, entrepreneurship requires discipline and a good dose of humour. Without these you could not look back (or forward for that matter) and examine your mistakes with the degree of sagacity necessary to move one foot forward without feeling despair, let alone plant another idea.

The beauty and power of winter lies in its serenity. During this time, you might feel exposed and at your most vulnerable, but it has more to teach you than any other season of business. All businesses are organisms and, as such, they are never silent—they speak volumes. A business takes the energy of your passion and the energy of those working in it and traps it into a bond that grows to create an impressive body with a life of its own. It becomes an entity with its own character, flaws, and merits, its own need for balance and a voice. Listen.

Typically winter is a turning point for many entrepreneurs. It is a time when things seem not worth the effort and the towel is thrown in prematurely, as I once did with my marketing business. But it can also be a time to press on, leading the entrepreneur to find a way to protect themselves and their business from an environment with which they are still largely unfamiliar, and which therefore makes them suspicious of organic growth. Business is about *not* doing as much as it is about doing, and for the go-getter entrepreneur, this piece of reality can be the source of some serious angst.

Business—*busi-ness*—the word itself is in direct opposition to the winter season. If we look at the meaning of the word business, it signifies "work," "busy," or "anxious." I know that this might seem counterproductive to some people, but when you are in the winter, the season is asking you to do exactly the opposite of everything you *think* business represents. It is asking you to slow down, to stop being busy or anxious about outcomes of whatever you are working on.

In the winter of your business, you are on the cusp, you're halfway between the old and the new world. By the time you've entered into winter, you've pretty much done all you could do with what you knew at the time, so relax and enjoy winter for the wonderful driver that it is. You're about to be stretched.

During the winter, you'll notice a decided sluggishness in your energies—you might procrastinate about everything and want to sleep more and hide while things just seem to s-l-o-w d-o-w-n. Growth is halted. It is time for rest and repose. Things are frozen and your efforts and actions may seem frozen as well. Everything you do seems to take twice as long. Survival in itself seems a cruel and wicked game. Responses in general—yours and those you're antic-ipating—seem to be running on molasses time. Your main theme seems to be "I'm out of synch," and you run the risk of singing that tune for the rest of this cycle if you do not listen and act accordingly. It is human nature to struggle and be willful when there is no movement, and at this time such force could be detrimental. In the winter, you will learn patience and that there is an influence greater than your own—which is nature, and this includes your natural rhythm. It's a time to honour your own rhythm.

But before you decide to end the life of your business out of sheer frustration, take a moment to realize that this is the natural course of the business cycle. And part of your job is to realize just what the rhythm of your business *feels* like. The winter of your business is not so much about get-ting in tune with all the elements that make up your outer world—printers, publicists, suppliers, journalists, business contacts, etc.—as it is about getting in touch with your per-sonal and inner world. Connecting and reconnecting again with your family and with yourself, gaining even greater familiarity with the core reasons for why you got into *this* business in the first place means reacquainting yourself with your Greater Purpose.

Many of us feel our lives are out of balance, and this is especially true for an entrepreneur—that individual who often tries to juggle the expression of passion, creativity, and profit in the form of a business with a second job, a family, and time to themselves. But if you heed your win-ters and honour them, then this balancing act can happen naturally, one can say even effortlessly, *if* we stop long enough to accept and appreciate the importance of the growth happening so close to home—within you.

Greater Purpose – The Soul of Your Business

What is your Greater Purpose and what does it have to do with business anyway? Everything. Greater Purpose is your unique reason for being on this planet. With a Greater Purpose, everything—your energy, your actions, and even your thoughts—has a conscious direction and a conscious effect. When you're aligned with your Greater Purpose, everything has meaning, importance, and significance. You see the whole map more clearly. Your Greater Purpose is what only *you* can do in this world. It satisfies and feeds the hunger deep within, but most of all it almost always involves the lives of many. You are always aware of ways to be of greater service to more than just yourself and your family. You realize that everything you do, touch, think, and set into motion has far reaching effects and will leave imprints on many levels of *being*, and so you are aware of each action your business engages in and what it stands for and how it conducts itself in the world.

Business is just one other system of energy. That's right, a system, nothing more and nothing less. It's another form of expression of a divine reality, a reality of thoughts, ideas, and information expressing themselves into an energy formation that manifests as the structure known as business. What do I mean by that? I mean that it is a collection of information and wisdom that organizes itself into alignment with whatever it is focused upon. This knowledge then leaves us asking a fundamental question, namely, what, then, is a system? One definition of a system is a condition of harmonious, orderly interaction, a group of many energy forms that are interdependent, interrelated, and interacting along a complementary structure. And, again, what does this have to do with business and Greater Purpose? When a business has no greater purpose other than making money or the gratification of its owner, then that energy system is misaligned, resulting in confusion and its general deterioration.

Often when I speak of Greater Purpose, most people get a glazed look in their eyes or feel bereft because they haven't *found* it or don't *have* it yet. But that is not the point. The relationship with one's Greater Purpose isn't so much about finding or having something as it is about coming into greater alignment with your Source.

Your Source is that place deep within you that feeds all of you. It is the master generator of all your actions, thoughts, and feelings. Some call it God; others call it the Universe or their Higher Selves. It doesn't matter what you call it; we all have it and relate to it to a degree. The diagram below shows us all the pieces that may or may not make up our lives—career or business usually being a very big part.

Typically, all the pieces are scattered everywhere and we're constantly jumping from one to the other with no real sense that they connect or are communicating with each other. This is not only ineffective and inefficient, but it doesn't make sense to mismanage our energies this way and adds to our sense of imbalance. Yet somehow, even with the seeming randomness, no matter how misaligned one's life is, the essence of our Greater Purpose *is* there, guiding, molding, shaping, directing. It lies at the heart of disorder; it's the regulator of unruliness and revolution, the architect of intelligence sprung from the imbroglio of life. As James Gleick writes in his book *Chaos: Making a New Science*, "…the greatest generator of information is chaos…" There's no need to fear it because Greater Purpose will balance it out; it's up to us to reshape our perception of chaos and recognize the gift inside the madness.

We all speak of businesses today lacking integrity. This is because the individuals that form the organizations have lost sight of their Greater Purpose, and so many businesses end up being a mere shadow or shell of the greatness they are meant to share with the world.

Your Life In-formation Before Alignment with Greater Purpose

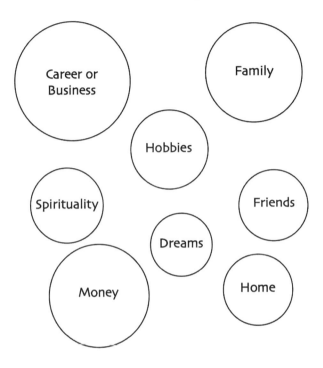

Looking at the image of alignment in the next diagram, notice that the size hasn't changed much from above, when they were misaligned. But now that the individual is aware of a Greater Purpose, the pieces somehow are in-*formation*, following a clear path. And as we progress along this path in business and in life, the amount of information we are able to access and assimilate in order to allow greater transformation and growth increases. This is why there cannot be transformation of businesses without the transformation of ourselves in the process, and at the heart of this process is your Greater Purpose.

It's as if we've always had CDs but only used them as coasters, and then suddenly find out that, "Hey! I can actually put stuff on here and share it with loads of people!" The same applies to the potential relationship between people and enterprise. When our passion, ambition, and skills are channeled through Greater Purpose, everything expands, giving us focus, abundance, improved communication, and thriving communities.

When business is imbued with Greater Purpose, there is an exponential growth in gratitude, greater insight, greater care (of self, others and the earth), and greater information, which increases the need for more highly effective communication.

Your Life In-formation After Alignment with Greater Purpose

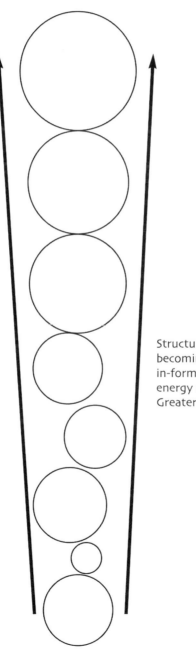

Structure formed by becoming aligned or in-formation with the energy system of Greater Purpose

The challenge we face in building businesses as organic entrepreneurs is to have the courage to embrace this aspect of Greater Purpose wholeheartedly. Sometimes the term alone can seem overwhelming. We instinctively want to reject it simply because we think we don't know it. We ask ourselves, "What if I'm lacking purpose to begin with, or "What if I find it and it isn't *great* at all?" You should take care not to judge or compare your Greater Purpose to anyone else's. The term *Greater Purpose* simply means your *highest* purpose possible, and that will always change as you grow and become transformed, making your Greater Purpose continuously unique and your products and services authentic.

Values – The Heart of Your Business

If Greater Purpose is the soul of your business, then the place where the soul rests is in the arms of values. When choices, which determine our course of action, are born from our core values, they become our life foundation. When our business actions are rooted in our deepest values, they become the heart of our business. Through your personal core values, your Greater Purpose finds tangible expression. Together, they form a safeguard. They will guide you through industry landscapes littered with lawsuits, avarice, and the temptation to grow without conscience. Values ensure that the choices you make are meaningful and grounded.

Values help to maintain the integrity of the soul of business. It is by adhering to these values, which influence the entrepreneur's life and business, that business will be able to take its next quantum leap. Once we've come to realize that the cost to the soul is too great, that a simple act of cutting costs or increasing revenue without mindfulness of the far-reaching shadows they cast, longer even than our life or the life of our business, then that is when we will awaken from the fool's slumber and take responsibility of the gift we've been given to co-create with a force much greater than our collective imaginations.

Your values serve not only as guideposts along the way, but also as beacons for your clients and for other business-es that you may want to interact with in the future. They become demarcation points that clearly say what you're about and what your clients can expect of you. I believe all potential employees should have clear in their minds what their own values are when walking into an interview. Furthermore, the current employees have an obligation, when asked by candidates, to clearly articulate both their own personal values and those of the business—the two should be closely aligned.

In order for this to happen, something else must take place: we need to be unapologetic about our values. There needs to be no shame in saying, "For now, I value ambition and money." The problem arises when we try to hide it, sugar coat it, or pretend that it's something else, that we're giving the customer more than what they're getting, lie that we're really about customer service when we're really only about personal gratification and wealth accumulation. Many of us were taught at a young age that the pursuit of money is wrong and that there's something extremely sus-picious about people who are wildly successful and have their dreams fulfilled. We have a right to value what we value, even if it is self-indulgence. I say this because the sooner we can allow ourselves and each other to experi-ence our chosen states of consciousness (without causing harm to others), the sooner we can move past material growth and on to something even more rewarding for our-selves and for the planet as a whole.

I believe that disagreements between individuals that cause separation, even wars, are fought in the hearts, minds, and spirits of individuals long before they ever become an outer reality that seduces whole countries. The disagreements I'm talking about are between our values and our fears, and this results in our minute-to-minute choices—every day, good or bad, productive or destructive. At the end of the day, our choices must sum up our values and not our fears. Will you go ahead and process an order for the full price just because a customer isn't aware that you have a 25% discount going on? You're strapped this month and you have an outstanding advertising bill due immediately: will you keep a double payment that a client isn't aware they've made to your company? The choice is always yours, but you'd better become more aware about what drives those choices and begin giving yourself better tools to fight this inner war. As organizations, we have the might to build great empires, but the wisdom, awareness, and love to manage them doesn't yet match our might— we're way off. Business is one of the most splintered territories, where the camps are very strictly divided between profit and purpose, values and revenue. But why the separation at all?

This separation exists because of the fundamental way that we've been looking at the world for over 300 years. A part of the cause of our splintered nature can be ascribed to the Newtonian science that we've all been taught, which, when synthesized, states that we can only truly know a thing by studying its parts—such a viewpoint assigns greater significance to the pieces than to the whole. And so we've been stuck focusing on the parts and are only now awakening to the wisdom that indeed a thing can be known just as well by contemplating the whole. The Newtonian paradigm has its importance and its limits and we are now seeing the effects of some of those limits. An organic entrepreneur desires to see things both in their parts and in their whole.

Secrets and Surprises

The winter of your business is about reconnecting with yourself, your family, and the fundamental structure of your business. Now is the time to figure out or concretize your reasons for being in business or what your business feeds in you. Even if one reason is ultimately to give you financial freedom, also remember that you should build a business to give you solace *and* surprises. You should always leave room to be surprised by what your business grows.

Winter is a time to sit back and enjoy the successes of the year from a safe, detached distance. During the summer and autumn seasons, when things are growing and you're harvesting the fruits of your labour, you often don't have the time to take a breath and acknowledge the great job you've done, the hurdles you've jumped, and the milestones you've passed. In winter, you can do this without the threat of being swept away by emotion and losing your head or your direction.

Your business, like a garden in winter, will also have its secrets—things you can't possibly foresee, and maybe that's a good thing. One of the secrets of my business that was hidden from me for the longest time was the way all these aspects of my life, my patchwork quilt of experiences, have served my marketing intuition as well as my ability to relate to a large, dynamic set of people at any given time. I couldn't see the beauty of the design of my own quilt because, truth be told, I love expensive bed sheets and can't stand quilts. Now I see that the life of a business doesn't always grow in neat little Beatrix Potter–like rows; sometimes it's a patchwork. Sometimes it's chaotic, but no matter how abstract, there is order in the design.

Winter is also a time when it's so easy to scare yourself silly, but there's no need to worry. Many people who love what they do during the other seasons of their business start hating what they do or become skittish about the business side of things during the winter. It's a time when attention to detail calls and the call must be answered in order for the business to stay healthy. Dealing with the nitty-gritty of business in winter is no different from dealing with the daily details of your life: you have to exercise, brush your teeth, and comb your hair everyday, or you start losing friends as well as teeth.

This season helps us become better listeners. During the silence—the lull—everything is muted, the volume gets turned down, and you can finally hear yourself think and feel the pulse of your business beating a rhythm. Do you hear it?

How does one *listen* to one's business? It's not what we listen to but what we listen *for*. You're listening for dissonance, for discord, for harmony, for joy, and for the quality of the purpose that drove you to start in the first place. Do this because after the initial launch, by the time winter rolls around, it's not that plainly heard. At times, it could almost be silenced, but it's still there. You're listening for your reactions to the way things are currently. Are you satisfied with this year's marketing efforts? Are you okay with the sales figures? Is one part of your life shouting louder than another? If so, when do you plan on dealing with it and bringing balance to those troubled areas? Listening to your business and how it intertwines with the rest of your life is about getting in tune with your environment.

So what does one *do* in the winter? The desire is there to pull the whole thing out by the roots—and this could be your hair—but you must exercise your will in an area other than your business at this time: your self. You must slow down. You are in the phase of reflection, dreaming, and deeper questioning. Now is the time to pull out those ideas (both old and new) and begin exploring different opportunities that you didn't have the time for during the other seasons.

Let your imagination take you to new heights, past what you think is possible and what you successfully accomplished this year, to places you never dared dream of. This is the time to start researching possibilities, making enquiry calls, gathering support. If during the other seasons, you were fearful of having only one key client who could walk out of your business and put it in trouble, now is the time to strengthen sales by exploring other potential clients or other avenues of your business that might be undervalued. You could dig up an unexpected opportunity and add another stream to your total income.

Let's say you are a landscape designer and you had a brainstorm during the summer for a specially designed underground sprinkler system that you could sell for much more than the average system. Well, now is the time to explore its feasibility. This is the sort of intentional dreaming I'm talking about. During the months when business is hopping, we don't have time to explore these avenues, but we do and we must during the winter phase.

Now is the time for actions such as:

Sending out thank-you notes

The little things people have done to make your business more fun or profitable should always be acknowledged with a thank-you note; it's like the grease that makes things run more smoothly and it helps maintain the constant flow of operations and abundance.

Backing up your files

This is not a simple task and not one to be taken lightly. You won't know how important this is until you no longer have access to important files, phone numbers, and contacts. For your first backup, I suggest you hire a techie to show you how it's done and then you should be able to do it on your own because the process is usually automated. You should do a complete backup once every three or four months thereafter, depending on your rate of growth. Once you've started backing your files up, check to make sure that they *are* actually being backed up, that the right files are being backed up, and that they are being backed up to the right hard drive.

Responding to e-mail

When things are harried, most of us tend to answer only the most urgent e-mails, but now's the time to go through those industry newsletters that are chock full of great ideas and information that you can use.

Renovating your website

Notice I didn't say "reconstruct" because people tend to like to see the same things but with just a few changes. Renovating is also done a piece at a time, so hopefully during the year you made notes of which areas you want to change. Now you can go through these notes and really get down to some serious reorganizing of your web content. You can redesign your landing pages to improve sales at the checkout. You can redo the content so people are better led through the site to exactly where they want to get with the minimum of clicks. The possibilities are endless, but the general idea is don't try and do it all at once, do it a "room" at a time.

Planning next year's newsletter

A newsletter is a great way to stay in touch with your clients and customers. The operative word in that sentence is *touch,* and that's what you need to do with your style of writing: you need to find ways to touch their spirits to create a bond that makes introducing new products or services easier.

If you plan the next twelve topics for the year, it makes it simpler when you're sitting in front of the computer, willing the creativity to leap forth. If you're not so good with words why not hire a writer for a few short hours a month to help you with the flow?

Planning next year's marketing campaign

As with any plan, there's always some sort of tweaking required. Since good marketing is based on the insights derived from experience, we sometimes forget to integrate these insights into the next plan of action. Did more people come through your business via the web or via referrals from customers? You might find that you should be putting more efforts towards rewarding referrals, increasing referrals, etc. All the little gems you've acquired over the past months are priceless pieces in the foundation of the success of future efforts.

Taking another look at management

This is a lot like taking inventory of your soul. If you're a single-person operation, then this process involves soul searching: finding out where your strengths and lesser strengths are and whether you are leading the vision of the company from a place of powerlessness, abundance, or love. If, instead, your business is comprised of a small team, then it requires searching the soul of the company for the same sorts of things. It's a time to ask, "How do I respond to crisis, to change, to new ideas that aren't mine?" Maybe attending a course on leadership would be a good idea during this time.

Engaging in research

Research leads to information, and a company can't survive very long without information. Information helps you feed your business both effectively and economically. It helps you be more agile and flexible. It also helps you realize before it's too late if you need help. You know the saying: the more you know the more you realize you don't know.

Now's the time to catch up on those industry trend magazines, take in some of those industry networking groups, and just open yourself up to absorbing the changes that have been happening in your sector. Also, start researching your in-house content in the form of company data. Start mining the information already contained in your databases to help you build a better sales and marketing system.

Tying up any loose ends

It's amazing how many entrepreneurs let go of certain aspects of their lives that don't have anything to do directly with their business. Friends have been repeatedly turned down, mail hasn't been replied to in a while, or maybe personal bills haven't been paid. Just remember that business is life and without life, we can't have a healthy business future.

Taking stock

Note the supplies and equipment you'll need soon. Is the fax machine or printer dying? If so, get them fixed or replaced. Do you need more help around the office so you can have more of a life? Then think of hiring a virtual assistant. Also take stock of the things you do have: a partner that supports your dreams, kids that are still a major part of your life, customers that believe in your product and trust you. They're all inventory and they're all assets just like the repeat customers.

Take the time to read

Just about everyone has a book that they can point to and say, "This has changed how I looked at business forever!" For me, that book is *Growing a Business* by Paul Hawken, founder of Smith & Hawken. I found it in the bargain bin at a bookstore (every author's nightmare) and I have lovingly dog-eared, written, and smeared it all over to an extent that puts it beyond lendability (an author's dream).

Hawken's ability to elicit what's in the soil of business

sheds remarkable light on the process of business and the entrepreneurial mindset for me. To this day, I still use the book as a reference to refresh me on the basics. His message about simplicity and trusting yourself always resounds with something deep inside of me. I was stirred and I began entertaining the notion that I had it in me to make a business work and make a difference even if it took me a few tries to get it right.

As with the terrestrial season of winter, this time in business may make you feel the furthest away from the sun: you seem to lack inspiration, passion, and enthusiasm. This is the time to delve into ideas, plans, or projects you canned earlier to fuel the fire during the long winter season, to feed the soul of your business, so to speak. Keeping the passion and spark alive can be a challenge during a time when there are no new clients knocking on your door. Stay close to your sun by giving your business the attention it needs from the inside out. We'll explore how to do that further along in this section.

Being prepared for the downtimes in your business can save you a lot of time and worry. Preparation is important because of the inherent rhythm and purpose of this phase: it lays things bare, making any holes in your business structure painfully obvious. Keeping focused during the wintertime can be tough. Sometimes the hardest lesson to learn is the realization that your business is still growing underneath all that ice and snow—you are still moving *forward* even though everything seems to be asleep or dead. This is because winter was designed for dreaming.

Dreaming Your Business Awake

Dreaming should be a prerequisite to building anything. There should be classes in dreaming because it helps prepare us for the possibilities. Here are some guidelines on how to dream your business into being before you start the work:

Get quiet

Spend quiet time sitting in a favourite place. Get comfortable. Begin to visualize your business. What do you see? Are you happy with what you see? What do you wish you *could* see through the window of your imagination?

Start wishing

Start with the vision. Dream big. Now dream bigger! Don't just accept bottom line answers like "my dream is for an increase in productivity by 20%" or "I want to make $300,000 profit this year." These are fine dreams, but stretch yourself. Imagine your ideal business. My own dreams in the beginning ranged from the desire to reach a certain income with the least amount of struggle to wanting to find a way to build a business that would eventually become a foundation for a bridge that could cross the financial divide that threatened to separate me from my self, my dreams, and other people.

The beautiful thing about wishing is that some wishes do come true. Start applying certain values such as time, freedom, authenticity, or whealth—a healthy relationship with money on all levels: spiritual, mental, emotional, and material—to various elements of your business. Don't try to think too much of the details of your plan yet. Right now, you want to be thinking about the "bones" or the underpinnings of your business, and these are your values, vision, Greater Purpose, and mission. The plot of your business garden might look something like this:

Start out with your values:

This vision slowly develops into this:

Before I drew this out on a chart, the business I envisioned looked like this: Maxine Hyndman—writer, speaker, coach. Full stop. There was no room for the IT side of things (a minor passion of mine) or the desire to have creative control over some of my publications. Now any brilliant idea I have for a project must fit within the above values or it gets put on the back burner to simmer and develop. This design grew completely organically out of my dreams and what I was good at.

It's a lot easier to see where things belong after you are clear about your framework or map and have marked out the spaces you want to nurture and grow into. With your framework, you can look at your business as one big integrated whole. You probably won't want to jump on the whole thing at once. In fact, you'll more than likely want to choose one area each year to focus and develop more broadly. At least now you have a visual plan.

Craft your story

Remember all the best businesses you've ever loved and admired: your favourite café, grocer, bookstore, or software company. Dig through your business magazines and find all the stories of companies that have ever inspired you. Ask yourself why they inspire you. What's compelling about their story? What have been the moments that have impressed you when dealing with other companies? When were you made to feel special by a company? Of all the businesses that you've seen, what would be the most important elements you'd like to adopt into your business? What's your company's story?

Now think of all the businesses you'd like to work for if you weren't an entrepreneur

What is calling you there? Their corporate culture, their lounge, their resource area? How can you use this as inspiration to cultivate your own environment?

Make a list of all the elements you've discovered

To help develop your dream business, you want to find the visual images or words that represent all the elements and then make a collage (one page only) out of old magazines and put it where you'll see it every day as a reminder.

During this exercise, don't be worrying about money, expertise, labour, your skill level, or your education. It's likely that you won't be able to source them all, but now is not the time to be confining yourself to what you think you know for sure. You will come to surprise yourself at how much you *can* accomplish if you give yourself permission to explore the possibilities unhampered by your fear or practicality.

The whole picture of all the elements of my business that I would develop over time jumped out at me from a chart I had posted on my wall. It was at this pivotal moment that the concept of the communications group fell into place, and I was shocked by what I saw. How could I possibly create something like this vision that was revealed in an instant? The more I began to build with a commitment and from my true values, the more I began meeting and invisibly creating the network of people, learning, events, thoughts, etc. that were the "missing" pieces that I needed. My life changed dramatically because of dreaming on a bleak winter day.

Goals to Grow By

We all need goals that will inspire us and challenge our preconceived beliefs. Time being what it is, you may not be able to achieve all of your goals this year or the next but I'll bet that what you do accomplish will be far greater than if you hadn't dared to dream at all.

In winter, everything seems possible and dreaming is a

serious part of business. This is a time when we spend more time looking at our business than being in it, but it requires an iron will to keep things in perspective.

To help sow the seeds of your dream business (whether you're mid-way or just beginning), the next process is a list exercise to help you create goals or variations of goals you would never have thought about yet have much to do with your business. It's a bit more left-brained, but it shouldn't limit your passion and is designed to challenge and expand your current expectations.

1. Make a wish list of your favourite office elements, the business contacts you'd like to meet and collaborate with, the type of office staff you want to be surrounded by, favourite projects you would love to work on… Don't hold back. Just list them.

2. Make another list of all the things you want to do with your business. Here are some ideas to get you started: I want to play hard, leave a mark of my love, build a foundation, build multiple streams of income from this core business, make this a fun place to spend eight hours a day, travel on business, get awards, get recognized by my industry.

3. If you feel the need, go ahead and make a list of the things you *don't* want in your business. The things you don't want may require you to make a lot of hard choices and, of course, will require time to weave them into the fabric of your business. Finding balance takes saying no to jobs or projects at times when your bank account says you must say yes. In my business, I personally like to be busy in large chunks of time and then take large chunks off time off—that's my balance.

4. Make a list of things you need in your business both structurally (such as space, a reading lounge, original artwork) as well as values and essential qualities (such as the sound of running water). You could draw some ideas from your values. Readers of my first book, *The Naked Millionaire*, are already familiar with the purpose of values and building a life around them. Values are things such as friendship, integrity, connectedness, tradition, fun, just to name a few.

I'll never forget walking into a flower shop on a very cold winter day. This shop in Toronto was unlike any other I've ever been in. The whole front, including the door, was made of iron and glass. When I walked in, I immediately felt invited, as though I would be asked if I wanted a cup of tea. What struck me most was the shopkeepers' easy camaraderie and lightheartedness as they each went about their work. Over in one corner was a beautiful sitting area surrounded by, of course, an amazing flower arrangement. That's the way I want my company office to be when we eventually grow into our own space and out of my home office.

After you've finished, take a break to let the soil settle and the plan take hold. Have patience, an important ingredient in winter.

Patience

Grow, grow, grow, already! As entrepreneurs, we buy the office equipment, we read all the business books and magazines we can get our hands on, we even get our own printed letterhead and envelopes, maybe even a first client or two. And then sadly, with rough impatience, everyday we yank our fledgling enterprise out by the sprouts, looking to see if the roots have begun to take hold. The pain of being an entrepreneur can be unbearable at times. Why am I still putting more into this thing than it's giving me back? Why can't I afford the time or money to go on vacation this year? Why haven't I gotten any referral business after two years!

Business is about purposeful activity. But if that's all business is about, then why is it so damn hard to wait for profits, to wait for more clients to run through the door when we've done everything we can to tell them out there about us in here? Oh, yes, that's right, the business books forgot to mention that business takes a mountain of patience—more patience than money.

In the beginning when I started with my first business, I rented office space. I spent nearly $1,000/month of money I didn't have, borrowing it from my home rent, to pay for letterhead and envelopes and office space. I told friends and family that I was open for business and what a great thing I was up to. Everyone was so excited and pleased for me. And then I waited by my phone, at my desk, in my empty office, day after endless day. Waiting.

As my nervousness grew, I went networking to build business contacts and develop leads, but because I had so much invested in the venture, I had painted myself into a very narrow, little corner with no room for mistakes or things to grow. I couldn't afford the one thing I needed the most in the beginning: patience. It had become an expensive commodity that I couldn't source.

In gardening, it's common practice to make sure the soil around your plants is *loosely* packed. Gardeners do not apply 100 tons of pressure to the dirt around their plants in fear that they will miraculously grow out of their containers, or sprout wings and take off. No, they pack the soil lightly and wait patiently. I had packed my own soil too tightly, leaving no room to grow, no room to breathe. This is why patience is so important and is an essential ingredient to be included in any marketing plan.

We all know what it means to be patient in a general sense, but most of us are reluctant to embrace and follow through with what this means on a day-to-day basis when building a business. What if we really don't need to experience the pain of growing a business? What if patience is about being ready—possessing the know-how and willingness—for the *possibility* of bearing pain? And what if being patient means we just need to be willing and able to bear what it takes to be in business? Are you patient? Are you willing and able to bear (possible) pains, opposition, difficulty, or adversity unlike you've probably ever known, from others as well as yourself? I often think they should give out business licenses with a notice that reads, "Warning! You will be tested! The contents of what you're about to create could evoke things within you that you may not be *willing* or *ready* to deal with!"

The amount of physical pressure that it takes for nature to create a diamond, for example, is similar to the internal pressure it takes to polish personal character. For me, being in business, among other things, has severely tested my patience—the character trait of mine that needs the most polishing. My patience has been and will be tested until I let go and am at the point where I no longer resist *being willing* to bear the *possibility* of pain for what I choose to manifest.

Especially throughout the winter, we are impatient with and have a reluctance to embrace the things that take time. But it cannot be ignored (do so at your own peril); business takes time to develop. You set your ideas down, print out your business cards, and buy your office equipment, and then six to twelve months later, you still may not be breaking even or breaking new ground. With ideas in business, you are always planting for the future—at least one or two years down the road. Resistance, in any form, to this concept is futile. The best remedy is to learn to love the process—even the mess.

Important Observations in Winter

Winter urges you to become an observer. When it comes to growing a business, taking the time to stand back and observe is just as important as taking action. Growing a business takes a sensitivity to all the things around you—to trends, markets, unexpressed needs—a sensitivity that has been much dulled by the experts and gurus, television, and the instant culture in which we live today. This doesn't mean that it is wrong to listen to those who may have greater knowledge, insights, or experiences than we do regarding a particular subject. I'm simply suggesting that these sources are not substitutes for our own experiences, insights, or knowledge relating to the very same subject. Experts are aids, not alternatives, to our own wisdom.

Growing your business is a co-creative endeavour. You must allow your business to be your teacher. Admittedly, this can be tough to do especially if you've approached your business with the intent to impose your own will upon it and anyone else who works for it. For instance, if you stubbornly want to promote a new service that the market just isn't buying, be prepared to pay the price. You need to be sensitive and remain conscious of what it is your market *does* want, *when* they want it, and *how* they want it. Furthermore, you need to be in tune with your rhythm to know when to develop this intuitive system.

This time of your business is actually the most creative and is the most crucial at the beginning because most of us have been taught—especially in business—that this quiet reflective time is a threat, that like a shark, we must keep moving, keep busy, or die. Think about it: during the rest of the year, you're mainly doing what you can do to carry out your dream's plan.

During the wintertime I try to stand back and ask a lot of questions about my business. What will it teach me this year? What have I learned from the previous year? The most important thing to observe in winter is yourself. A business always gives evidence of the spirit of the owner(s). What does your business say about you? Winter is the time to learn what you can about yourself and adjust your plan to any changes in character you need to make to allow for a more productive, satisfying business. Does it say that this year you need to read more, get back in balance, take a course in leadership or delegation? Whatever it is, take note to add it to the plan.

Creating the Structure – A Business Map

A business plan is not the same as a business map. A map is not as fixed as a plan is intended to be. A map shows many different roads leading to your destination. You may start out taking the scenic route or you may want to get there in the more direct way. Maps also give you the benefit of seeing things from a higher viewpoint, which is why including your Greater Purpose and values in your map is so important. They help you get above street level to give you a much more holistic perspective of your entire terrain.

Bringing your dreams to life needs planning, there's no getting around it. If you haven't already done so, take pen in hand and start drafting a business map, but keep it simple! I'll take you through the elements of one in a moment. If you already have one, then now is the time to take it out, dust it off, and give it a serious in-depth look. Here are some questions to ask yourself as you look through your map:

1. How does this map reflect where I am today in the business?

2. Do I have the resources (physical, emotional, mental, and spiritual) to take this business to the

next level? If not, how do I see myself attracting the right ones?

3. Do I have the necessary skill set to navigate through the map?

4. Do I still want to be in this business? Is it still a passion? If I'm in a slump right now, is it just a phase of my business or is it an exit signal?

5. What have I successfully navigated by following this map?

6. What needs to be reworked? Financial projections? Milestones? Marketing approach?

7. What am I not seeing? Am I too far away or too close?

To make your dreams a reality, you need a framework, or, as I mentioned before, a structure. But don't let this part get you down or make you feel overwhelmed, and please resist the urge to overthink or overplan the process. Remember, your soil needs room to breathe. Structure is necessary for dreams, it is not a curse upon creativity. It's a vital element that many entrepreneurs, creative beings that we are, neglect to factor into the design of our business.

Your job then is to create an outline of the bones of the business. Some people are conflicted in this phase because it forces them to choose and to focus their energies and desires toward a specific purpose, but we can't create without focus and clarity. Focus really is the prime ingredient in manifesting our dreams out of nothing, and this is especially the case in a business.

You certainly could create your dream business without a business map; many have done it—just jump in instinctually and get right into it. There is no right or wrong way to do this. It all depends on your style, your tolerance for risk, and your ability to handle unknowns. Personally, I've learned the value of a business map as a tool to corral my energies and as a compass. I've seen that it takes a certain level of readiness and awareness to build from a plan or map. Too much planning and you become plagued with inertia and doubt. Not enough planning could create a situation for dissipated energies and operating by the seat of your pants more times than not. Just imagine the stress this could cause. Either way, a map or framework is especially useful if you need to communicate your ideas to another person such as your life or business partner, investors, or potential customers.

Here are the basic pillars of a business map framework; the rest can get filled in as you go:

Executive Summary

This is where you briefly describe your vision, mission, philosophy, and guiding principles—the reasons why you went into this business. Also state the various stages that your business naturally goes through, what experts you have at your service, and describe the nature of your business as succinctly as possible. This section should be no more than a page long.

Management

This is you in the beginning—your values, personal goals, and beliefs. It's the way you view the world—your market, your Greater Purpose, and the possible effects of your family life—as well as your role in it, both positive and negative. But it's also about the nitty-gritty details of managing your business day to day; collecting on overdue invoices, tracking mileage, following up on leads, asking for referrals, and making decisions. How good are you at developing the muscle that allows your inner voice to speak its truth about an important decision? Especially when the decision is hinged on fiscal imperatives, this takes courage, a willingness to communicate outside of your comfort zone, patience, and love.

Marketing and Sales Strategy

How do you intend to get your product or service to the public? What's your price point? What's your edge, what makes you different (i.e. what's your U.S.P. – Unique Selling Proposition)? Who comprises your market? Describe them in great detail. For example, do they read the *Globe and Mail* or the *Wall Street Journal*, or *People Magazine*; are they typically single or married with children? The more you can say about them in detail, the better prepared you are to recognize them and take action if you meet them at a party or in the bank line, for example. I always tell my coaching clients that they should know what their ideal customer looks like, even from 100 yards away.

Potential Ancillary Products/Services

Don't put all your eggs into one basket, and don't leave yourself or your business vulnerable to being crippled by one negative impact. To plan for this, make sure you think about spinoff products or services, just like the University of Waterloo spun off not only Research In Motion (the creators of the BlackBerry) but also a host of other high-tech, high-yield businesses.

Spinoffs are a buffer to protect your sales in the event of economic downturns in your sector. If you own a spa, a spinoff could be to create a line of shampoos and conditioners. If you design websites, a spinoff could be to develop software that helps other developers with common problems you've encountered time and again. But, more important, if you're seeking funding, including spinoffs in your business plan shows forward-thinking, preparation, growth value, and that your business is flexible and adapt-able to trends. That's the kind of business you want to be investing your time in, and that's the kind of business investors want to invest their cash in. How do you plan to build multiple streams of income from your core business? What products or services could you see being complimen-tary by-products of your core business?

The S.W.O.T Analysis

Basically, this is an in-depth look at the unique Strengths, Weaknesses, Opportunities, and Threats that your business could face. To make it easy to digest, create a visual like the one below and fill it with bullet points that apply to your enterprise. If there's a section that you feel needs special mention, then expand on that.

Strengths

- What edge does your company come in with?
- What do you do better than anyone else?
- What common resources do you have the ability to transform into valuable ones?
- What do others in your market consider your stengths?

Opportunities

- Where are the good opportunities facing you?
- Why are they opportunities?
- What are the interesting trends in your industry that you are aware of?
- Do you have the personal and business resources to be able to take advantage of them?
- Do you need support taking advantage of them?

Weaknesses

- In what area are you most uncomfortable stretching?
- What could you improve?
- What personal traits or business actions are best avoided?
- What are people in your market likely to see as your weaknesses?

Threats

- What personal or business obstacles do you face?
- Who are your competitors and what are they doing?
- Are the requirements for your products or services changing, e.g regulations, certification etc.?
- Is the struggle to keep up with technology threatening your position?
- How healthy are your personal and business finances?
- Could any of your weaknesses seriously undermine the life of your business?

Financials

We'll get into money and the way you and your business relate to it in more detail in spring, but for the purpose of creating a map, we're talking about an overview, a snapshot of how well greased the mechanics of your business are. This is the part where you consider and plan your income projections and cash flow. This shouldn't become an Alan Greenspan–type document addressing the nation about financial forecasts. Keep it simple and truthful. Money is such a liquid thing that it's hard to try to pin it down sometimes, and it could seem the more you try to get a solid hold—without a couple years' experience behind you—the more elusive it becomes. Just try to be as honest with yourself as possible as you project into the future what you already know you can and cannot commit to financially.

Exit Strategy

Not many business plan primers talk about this, but to me the ending is just as important as the beginning; it's as vital a consequence to ponder as the decision to jump in. Here you'll be asking yourself things like: How do I want to remove myself from this business when I'm all done? Do I see myself moving on to something else, handing it over to a family member, selling, or staying on the board and bringing in a CEO, for example? Doing this gives you a sense of control over how you want to leave and avoid being pushed out or run over by the next crew that plans to take over.

Personal Environments – An Introduction

There's something else that needs to be taken into consideration that isn't really touched on during the typical process of business planning and that is your personal environment. Your personal environment is a combination of everything that makes up your world: your thoughts, your living space, your workspace, the people you interact with. It is everything that surrounds you that affects, moulds, and creates your circumstances or conditions. We rarely stop to notice all of the elements in our lives that touch us even subtly, they just seem to merge into one thing called "your life." When we add the element of consciousness, interacting with the things that stimulate us intentionally, we begin to design them for self-empowerment. This way, we become comfortable with those processes that we simply take for granted, whether they be our actions, our mental processes, or our personal habits.

But why is it important to factor personal environment into the business planning equation? Simple. It's because it is everything. It's where you are planted. It's probably where you're going to spend the most time if your business is successful along the current path. But you run into trouble if you don't like where you are right now because the odds are you won't like doing what you're doing five years from now. The solution is to focus on your environment and make subtle changes that enable and enhance a more conducive flow of energy that supports your dreams, actions, and thoughts. (I'll cover more on energy patterns in the section on autumn).

Let me give you an example: "Michael" has just started a new business. He's bustling with new energy, but begins encountering new environmental challenges in his small, cramped living space—no room for the new fax machine, printer, and computer he's needed to purchase and definitely no room to see clients in. His current quarters just aren't in line with his new changes in energy flow made by the decision to go into business as a massage therapist.

One solution could be to carve out some workspace by adding screens or dividers in his largest living space. Another could be to "time share" some office space; that is by paying a small amount, say $50 to $100 per month, for the use of a desk, some office equipment, and a receptionist during certain times of the week. Another solution could have been to have all his electronics wireless and networked. This way, he could be working on a laptop from any room in his home, freeing him from wires and the confines of a small workspace.

Many of us jump into business and don't realize that we're stressed by the environments that we're currently living in and must change, even if minutely, the very way we are planted in our space and how we choose to be nourished by it. Deciding to go into business is like moving into a whole new home, but the move doesn't have to be painful.

Moving from the plan to reality can be quite a bumpy ride. It can be a lot like coming in for a landing during a plane ride, and as we all know, the landing and takeoff are the most risky moments in a flight. Here are eight easy steps to make your business take off smoothly:

Step 1 – Plant yourself where you are

Take your map and identify the natural environmental conditions you have to deal with. Issues may include:

- your spouse's attitude toward your endeavour
- your kids' schedules
- a part-time or full-time job
- budget constraints
- transportation
- Internet connectivity
- office equipment
- personal tendency to procrastinate
- personal tendency to be shy

Include personal character traits that you know could be impediments. Once, during a battle of wills with a business partner of mine, I began to withdraw emotionally from her and the business because I was beginning to grow in a different direction and needed a business that could expand with my creativity, and this wasn't it. If you know something like this of yourself, then don't plant yourself in a tiny niche that you can't grow out of.

What's important to know at this step is where you are in relation to your "sun." Just as in gardening, your sun is your energy source, the one thing you've come to rely on to nourish you and sustain you through the ups and downs of being an entrepreneur. Many problems can be avoided simply by knowing where your business is positioned in relation to your source of energy or passion. If a major source of your energy is derived from your family, don't spend too much time away from them. Maybe you draw energy from learning; if that's the case, then make sure you have ample opportunities to attend workshops, conferences, or courses throughout the year. You get the idea.

Step 2 – Know where you've been, know where you're headed

It's called testing your soil: check for "hazardous" elements or deficiencies in essential qualities that you know are necessary for your business growth and ultimately for success. Sit down and think about your history, your trials and triumphs, and what you're bringing to this business. What sort of headspace are you in right now? What sorts of challenges are unique to you or people like you? The more you can honestly assess your past actions, the better equipped you'll be to manage present and therefore future risks.

Thinking in terms of the future now, draw some lines in your mind, or on paper if you're more visual (like I am), to what would seem to be the product or service income streams that would be a natural fit. It is true that you do have control over yourself and your business, but if you allow the business to go too far from its core, or you from your Greater Purpose, then you end up with separation, loss of energy through confusion, or too steep a learning curve, resulting in the loss of momentum or desire. You want to grow *with* your business, so keeping inventory of who you are now and where you stand needs to always factor into your business design and redesigns over the years.

Step 3 – Mentally plot your boundaries and limits

Plot the various values that make up your life and person. For example: Vitality, Integrity, Connectivity, Generator, Tradition, Travel, Inspiration. Just get a sense of how far removed from these values you are willing to be before it starts to hurt you. I know, after years of trying, that I can take no more than about four days of spending time with friends before I find myself craving private time.

Next, take a look at the various aspects of your business: there's administrative work, marketing and networking, research and development, and sales and promotion. Each aspect of your business needs your attention at some point in the week or month. Decide how much you're going to dedicate to each and how long you can go without doing each task and then follow through. One can run the risk of getting too caught up in administrative activities as a way to avoid doing the sales and marketing.

Another example is getting wrapped up in creating new content and redesigning the website until months have gone by and little work has been done to drive sales, causing the well to dry up and then you find yourself scrambling. No one wants to be scrambling in business, doing so can drain your energy. To avoid such a state, simply set your boundaries by dedicating and following your chosen schedules.

Step 4 – Begin digging here

As you design your business map, notice too the direction in which your business has a natural tendency to grow. Let's say you want to open a clothing boutique but you've started getting a lot of sales for some pieces of jewelry you've been dabbling in. It would be wise of you to begin including your jewelry for sale in your shop or consider increasing the focus of your business on the jewelry.

Every business has its natural growth pattern. You can create the pattern or map for your business too, but sometimes those areas already naturally exist and they typically come with their own brand of magic. The beauty of business is that nearly anything you face comes in cycles and so the big question to ask yourself is: how do I weave my dreams into what I already have to make things better, more efficient, more productive, and more profitable.

Step 5 – Commit to your dream

Intent and commitment are the name of the game when beginning a business. Think for a moment about a tomato seed. It doesn't start out planted as a tomato seed and then change its mind as a seedling to become a tulip just because they're prettier and easier to grow. You have a dream, and the truth is that there will be some very hard moments. Some of these moments might come from your environment as you struggle to grow a business from old, outdated personal belief systems and realize you have to change your thought patterns to support a new consciousness.

Other challenges might come from the outer environment—friends, family, money, equipment, schedules, etc. It is during these times that your intent and commitment to the dream is challenged. You need to revisit the plan again and recommit from a different perspective if something major has changed.

Ideally, as an organic entrepreneur, you want to enjoy and find peace in all four seasons of your business, but winter seems to be the most ignored. Most people—both in gardening and in business—wish it would just hurry up and go away. But the winter season in business is the best time for spotting design and growth problems because everything is laid bare, your entire structure is exposed. Here are some structural issues to look for in winter:

- Check for early signs of overexposure or overextension.

- Check for balance between your private life and business life.

- Check that you've included a healthy mixture of your core values.

- Check to see if you still feel inspired, motivated, and passionate.

- Check to see if you still *like* the business you're in.

During the winter, ask yourself, "How can I create something useful, something resembling my dreams in my own 'backyard'? How can I weave what I *know* will work here and what I *need* to be inspired?" You'll be surprised at how quickly you get back on track and how much more energized you feel just by checking in.

Step 6 – Pick your projects with care

Now take your list of favourite things that you'd like to do and start putting them where they make sense on the wheel, like in the diagram we looked at earlier. The most important thing you can do to aid in your success as an entrepreneur is to plant the right project in the right place to begin with. It took me almost five years to see the picture of my business garden and plot everything I was building where it needed to be. For example, I realized that designing software was all about the value of inspiration for me. I'm always inspired by useful Information Technology, but I know I could never work in the field full time.

You could spend a lifetime planning a business and it still might never make it off the ground. You could also spend lots of time building the business and never have a finished map. A good business plan, like a good garden, is never really finished because then there would be nothing left to dream, and what would the fun be in that?

The ability to enjoy and reap all of the benefits of the winter season of your business lies in your state of mind or rather your state of acceptance. During this time it's so easy to complain about the decline in sales or lack of inspiration and avoid the map. Familiar doubts seem cosy to you like an old blanket in the cold. There are so many ways, I've learned, to turn that frustration and anxiety into a sweet, quiet joy. Here are some of my favourites:

• Search through the iStockphoto.com database for cool, cheap images to use in simple updates of your site or future e-mail campaigns.

• Sit quietly in a favourite place and watch the world speed by, thankful that you are able to consciously enjoy a rest.

• Take care of yourself and your health. Start a simple vitamin plan, make yourself and your family good healthy meals, start exercising…again.

• Subscribe to and explore magazines that have nothing to do with your industry; this can be a great catalyst to creativity.

• Take a course in something that has always intrigued you and is completely different from what you do.

• Meet with friends. Talk. Laugh. Truly enjoy their company and be grateful that they're still around despite your extended absences.

• Join a new group in your industry.

• Take a walk and take note of how many things you haven't noticed in your own "backyard" before.

• Plan for the conferences, tradeshows, and events you'd like to attend in the coming year.

• Plan a trip.

• Dream of the springtime of your business.

• Review the records of your progress: last year's financials, any press about your business, testimonials from clients, etc.

When we look at our business "garden" in winter, we see all of our mistakes: the lost opportunities to send out and follow up with press releases, the haphazard way that things were growing because of a lack of organization and planning, the wrong keywords chosen for your website which resulted in lower web traffic. But this is what business is all about—the good, the bad, and the ugly and how to manage the risks of each with wisdom and savvy.

Instead of focusing on what went wrong, one of my favourite things to do in winter is redesign my business from the ground up—in my head! It's a safe place to look at what I would have done had things been different; it's a safe alternative to pulling up everything by the roots and starting again with a whole different design. To compensate for this waywardness, I have now learned the benefits of working on tiny projects in different parts of the business at various times during the year. It limits the failures and keeps them much more private. I also choose to ignore different areas so that I'm not tackling more than I can manage (an entrepreneurial handicap). This helps eliminate many problems I wouldn't normally have the time or money to solve.

Business and the Alchemy of Self

Business is about the alchemy of self: our growth and change into higher states of self-realization. Alchemy is about personal transformation. If Greater Purpose is about aligning oneself in-*formation* with the divine, then business and the alchemy of self is about trans-*formation*, transposing old information into a new formation based on our growth of awareness of community, connection, and love.

Why do we build businesses? I am always asking myself and others this question and I get run-of-the-mill answers such as: "I like the control it gives me over my own time" or "I need to be there for my kids and feel more fulfilled" or the ever popular "I want to make more money." I know there's more to it than this. These are the literal, more obvious aspects to being self-employed.

If we dig deeper, we will find that business connects us to each other, to people we might never have met otherwise—business forces us to be clear on our dreams. In essence, if we use it for the tool it can be, business can connect us to a deeper level of our being. Whether people are aware of it or not, being an entrepreneur is like being an alchemist; it's about transforming ourselves and our skills—what we were originally given at birth—to attract and manifest abundance in all its forms through increased awareness. The process of business moves slowly, ultimately to change *us*.

To organically grow your business, you must realign all dimensions of your business to encourage it to function as a natural habitat. This involves restoring personal equilibrium among your values, goals, beliefs, Greater Purpose, and actions. Success is achieved when people of like minds want to invest, work, play, and learn in your "garden." Your job is to foster and nurture such growth so your business becomes this place.

As human beings, we would like to believe that we have control over our domain, our personal systems. As entrepreneurs, we particularly want control over our business systems. Much of our energy is used in willing things to be, to mould by sheer power of intention, and while this approach does have its uses and merits, the best use of the will during winter is over oneself. This means knowing when to hold back, to wait and observe what is taking place in your business—is the landscape changing? If so, when is the best time to change things and in which direction should you go? It becomes crucial in a small business because the use of one's will has far-reaching consequences in the confines of such a small playing field. This world we live in, just like our world of business, is a system that is profoundly interconnected. What is willed in one area of your operation will have consequences in another. Your job as an organic entrepreneur is to become sensitive to this system and govern your actions, thoughts, and emotions accordingly.

Discipline is the key to your conscious intent. This means making absolutely sure you think about your business as a habitat for you, your staff, and your customers during the design of a project. The future of business will require the conscious use of the will to engage in patient observation, meaning more time will be spent in quiet contemplation of what the business is offering rather than on spending high-octane energy to obtain instant results and to engage in more and more "busyness."

As an entrepreneur, you are scientist *and* artist; the longer you're in business, the more finely tuned your instruments of discretion, intuition, and creativity become. Understanding the principles of business mapping is a good foundation to have, but it is not essential for the creation of something that satisfies your needs. The lessons of business are mainly about attitude, teaching us not only about our environment but also about our own character flaws and power of spirit.

There's been a lot of ink spilled about the dismal state of big business lately. So many people see only the bad side of enterprise because, let's be realistic, it's not always pretty. It's a shock to notice in myself, as it was blatant in many business leaders, that over the years business has brought out in me (although I'm not alone) every one of these five passions of the mind:

- *Vanity* – when achieving some beguiling and ephemeral success, I would attribute it to me alone;

- *Anger* – at myself and the world if some idea of mine didn't pan out or wasn't fully embraced by the market;

- *Attachment* – to the material gain, be it money or accolades;

- *Greed* – when I railed at the heavens that there just wasn't enough—not enough profit, clients or press attention—and this after being published by the first publisher I sent my first manuscript to!

• *Lust* – when I could never find the time to be quiet and accept how far I've come and instead yearned always for more—more of what other successful authors had, more success.

The realization dawned on me that it wasn't the business that needed cultivating, it was me! My early experiences taught me that this knowledge cannot be learned solely from a book, the Internet, or a mentor, as important as they all are as tools. This epiphany could only be truly appreciated by rolling up my sleeves and getting dirty. When you're down and out, having lost money and time on a business opportunity that went horribly wrong, you become aware of where you didn't listen, of the moments you could have turned back but didn't out of pride or ego.

I believe this awareness is an integral part of business and part of being connected to the world through conscious creativity. This awareness is vital for the work ahead: healing the soul of business. To do this, we need organic entrepreneurs—entrepreneurs who are willing to be altered fundamentally by their businesses. And it all starts by listening.

Listening 101

We all think that we know how to listen just because we have two ears. This is not so at all. Listening happens internally as well as externally, and most of the time, we don't even connect the two. Listening is a tool we need in every single relationship we have in our lives—with ourselves, our Source, the environment, our money, our kids, our partner, etc. When it comes to listening, we've sort of cut ourselves off from learning better ways to listen simply because we think we already know how to do it. Remember, you can't teach an individual anything if they think they know it all.

So how do we relearn a life skill such as listening when we're under a false assumption that we know how to do it already? The answer is to do it consciously because most automated human functions are done unconsciously. Here's how to relearn the art of listening consciously as applied to business:

Listen with your body

Your body has its own wisdom and is constantly sending you messages. Listen and take care of it. Your body is able to sense types of subtle communications that are going on around you all the time. If you're exhausted because you've been pushing yourself for weeks but you still reluctantly drag yourself to your next meeting, you're not listening. Pushing yourself to the limits does not encourage balance and it's not taking good care of yourself. It also sets up an energy pattern of push-push-push that becomes difficult to break through when *you're* truly ready to dedicate the time.

Listen with your breath

We all know that we typically breathe much more shallowly than we should, ultimately taking in an insufficient amount of oxygen. When this happens, connections get dropped between what we hear and how we interpret the world. With more oxygen comes better concentration, meaning the brain doesn't need to make assumptions and communication flows much more easily.

Listen through your environmental signals

If you're considering taking on a business partner, for example, and you choke up, feel a shortness of breath, or any other disturbance every time you meet to discuss things, take a closer look at what might be underneath it all. Does it feel like you shouldn't be doing this? Are you feeling intimidated? "Listen" to all the unspoken things that are being said through what's happening—those things that are *not* being said that might be causing you unnoticed anxiety. Listening involves much more than hearing words; it's also about hearing the life that goes on around the words. It's the space between the beats.

Get centred in the present

If we remind ourselves to stay in the here and now, we won't be hearing things we *thought* the other person said while we were thinking about the missed recital or the future money we'll be making on a deal. Instead, we'll be hearing what's being said *now*. By being in the present moment, we can never feel that we've been controlled or deceived without our knowing.

Be flexible enough to change

Listening means being open to the possibility that you can reach your goal much more efficiently and positively than you could imagine. Be open to a nudge, a hunch, or an insight that could guide you in a different direction or cause you to halt for a bit.

Acknowledge that you are part of a greater whole

You are an important part, but a part nonetheless. If we've become full of our own self-importance, we may fail to listen with an open mind. Consuming self-importance may cloud the meaning of words that others are trying to communicate. Try to get out of the way when you're listening and you'll learn more than you ever thought possible without being in a classroom.

Accept

Listening well takes accepting that we probably don't have all of the answers. Scary, I know, but that's a fact when we listen. We don't always know exactly what point of view the other person is coming from. We all bring different backgrounds, cultures, and experiences into what we choose to communicate. If we can come to an acceptance that we don't have all the pieces yet, then business can start becoming a true collaboration from a higher vantage point.

Letting go

Now here's probably the most challenging part. Effective listening involves a lot of letting go of our own desires, perceptions, fears, and assumptions. Many in business miss amazing opportunities to make more money with better structured deals simply because they're much too wrapped up in what they're willing to lose, gain, or how it will make them look. Let it go. In order to let go and listen, you need to get out of your own way. You need to get out of your place of comfort and ease.

Comfort Zones

Let's be honest. For all the sexiness that a Ferrari offers, nothing beats being comfortable. We feel safe in our comfortable clothes, our comfortable home, our comfortable couch, and our comfortable relationships. We all love comfort because it doesn't test us and there are no expectations to continually exceed. But in business, a comfort zone is like driving off a cliff in that Ferrari.

Why is it so hard for us to move past the safety of a comfort zone, that place where we feel super certain, where we've made many clients and attracted amazing press coverage? Well that's because it's…comfortable.

What is a comfort zone? It's that place we feel we can't leave without the support of a huge helping hand. It's that place we never really thought we'd get to, but we surprised ourselves and now we're frozen. Well, what's next? We don't move a muscle for fear of losing the ground we've gained or the ground we know.

How do you get past this "block"? You know you're in it because everything you try just seems like you're spinning your wheels, but somewhere deep inside, you know that you have to get past it or you risk destruction. And no matter how long you've been aware of this position, you resist. In my business, comfortable is being in front of my computer, writing or developing workbooks or new software. For me, comfortable is *not* being out giving public talks or workshops or interviews. But I would be a fool to ignore these initiatives as they are the accelerants of my coaching practice.

While it would be easy for me to tell you to simply whip yourself out of this comfortable place, what you should realize is that it's important to express compassion for that little part of yourself that just loves comfortable— that part that doesn't want to grow. There's a small being within you that is still afraid to fail, afraid of criticism, afraid of not being liked. This little being is you just before you realize how much you can actually accomplish. It can also be the voice in a corporation that says, "This is how we've always done it; it's worked really well for us in the past, so we're just going to go with what's worked." Yes, this little being can be quite compelling; after all, it does make a good point, but it's time to meet the giant.

The giant is the very tiny voice that says, "You can do this. You can achieve this goal/dream, but you know what you need to do. You have to step out." The giant can accomplish so much, but it scares the dickens out of the little being. The giant can get you past your comfort zone, the little being cannot. Sure you can stop and rest here, in your comfortable place…but we all know what can happen to mountain climbers that want to stop and rest—they might never wake up again. So, please, celebrate your first really big client, your first listing on the first page of Google, your first mention in the *Wall Street Journal*, or that first celebrity client. Just don't get too comfortable with these milestones because if you're not careful, they could be headstones.

If you want comfortable on this journey, satisfy the little being and buy a really comfortable sweater, or wear jeans around the office—it really is cheaper in the long run.

God and the Devil Live Here

Where is this place you ask? This dreaded place is what most entrepreneurs call "the details." As entrepreneurs, some of us get lost in them, while others avoid them like the plague. Whether it's picking up your suit from the cleaners so you have something to wear to the talk this evening or checking and rechecking your press release for grammar and spelling errors, there's no getting around it, details are a vital part of thriving.

When I was in high school, I loved writing essays for my English classes, but I always dreaded doing the rough draft; I absolutely hated it! All I wanted was to express my thoughts, ideas, and creations, to get them out there and get the feedback—the quicker, the better. What typically ended up happening, though, was that the teacher couldn't get past the spelling errors caused by my overzealous nature long enough to enjoy the brilliant ideas that lay beneath it. And why should she have to work at getting past my spelling errors or incorrect grammar? My carelessness communicated that I didn't appreciate her enough to check my work before using her valuable time. As assignment after assignment was returned with a poor grade (which I felt my great work didn't deserve), I gave up and began hating the process of producing good work. I began to dislike writing.

It wasn't until I got into business that I realized that the rough draft is a valuable tool for ironing out the details, for getting the details right because either way, you're going to make an impression. Make sure you deal with the technicalities so that the impression you really want to make comes through unobstructed and clear. If you don't, your customers will make their own impressions and generally they won't be favourable.

I also learned that a rough draft isn't always written on foolscap paper; it comes in many forms. Dealing with the minutiae came in the form of giving the same pitch over and over again, answering the same questions over and over again during my first book tour. But each time I gave the pitch or answered the questions, my position became stronger, my answers came with more certainty and confidence, and I had the space to get past the words and become more engaged and have more fun. That book tour prepared me for BookExpo America, the largest book expo in North America (my final draft). By then, I was polished and nothing got in the way of my presentation.

Dealing with the nitty-gritty actually is a hidden step in the creative process that helps the end user effortlessly use what we have crafted. If we don't deal with them, it makes it harder for a potential customer to see the benefits. Cheat the devil if you dare, but don't cheat yourself by cheating on the details—you'll wish to God you hadn't.

Reflecting on the Season

We need businesses that engage the spirit, businesses that quietly declare and boastfully celebrate a connection with each other for profit and for purpose—businesses that inspire human beings to reach for their potential.

During the winter of your business, you can smell it; that some ideas you've planted are brilliant and are going to grow into something beautiful, but you're not yet prepared for the fact that it takes a while before you can tell what it's *really* going to be once it starts growing—or not. It's too early at this stage to make assumptions about the future based on successes of the previous year. Just keep growing.

Planting the seeds of your ideas will bring exciting surprises as you wonder in winter what will be born of your actions: a contract, a new service, a new market opening up. It is amazing how each aspect of the system will reach out and multiply until the sum of all its parts breaks out of any plan you had previously conceived.

Spring

Create what you will, covet what you want, desire what you see, but you, me, we are never fully born until we can serve as well as we take.

Holy Spirit help me to
have financial Freedom,
escape me from financial bondage
Listen to the prompting of the
Holy Spirit.

Spring's Creation

What seemed like an endless wait is now over. It's spring, and the wet ground seems almost to be alive. The air too seems alive and we tingle all over with expectation. We expect the commitment we had to our visions and ideas throughout the winter to come to something. We expect our patience during the darkness and the silence to be rewarded with creation, and we get that in spring.

"Let us out," everything cries, "We want to go out and play!" We've got boundless energy that feels like it's never going to end. The days are longer, and although there's more to do, we don't care; all that work only fuels our passion for creating even greater dreams. And so now our ideas have grown into visions that, imbued with their own energy, are seeking resolution and expression in our world. It takes enormous energy for a plant to break through the ground and this is just what we are experiencing, the jubilation and pain of finally breaking ground. Breathe it in and dig in—it's time to begin.

Spring, that time of business when you can just smell potential, is welcome like no other season, and nowhere is this sense of potential stronger than in the heart of the organic entrepreneur. You finally start to see some blossoming of your ideas even if you can't yet savour the fruits. Projects come alive effortlessly with the influx of connections, information, and sales. There's a huge exhalation after having been hemmed in by situations seemingly out of our control, and now we're ready because the potential that we are feeling is our willingness to merge our ideas with our Greater Purpose. It is conscious creation and it could only be organic.

Rebirth

As I come into spring in my business, I notice all of the tiny projects and opportunities that could allow me to expand and grow. In the beginning, they are just whispers of potential success; I wonder if they will even survive, their being so delicate and vulnerable. I'm always on the lookout for weeds—you know, those actions or strengths that could be hindering my business growth, like wanting to do everything myself or not being honest enough about how much money, energy, time, or passion I *actually* have to accomplish a goal rather than just dream about it.

When ideas in my mind are so new, I've learned to resist the urge to fuss over them too much and to pick at my weaknesses. This is the time when I take long walks and try to still my thoughts, which are sometimes my worst enemies…okay, I admit…most times. I worry about my ideas being "perfect," whether they will be healthy or prosperous or well received before they're even let loose! This is the wrong time to be having thoughts like these; we need to be much more gentle with the process of birthing ideas because they are very susceptible to the elements of our environment.

And then there are those wonderful plans you've crafted during the winter months—all the new ideas to consider, contacts to develop, and organizations to join. This is the time when it is okay to admit they all looked perfectly fine on paper but now they do seem a lot more daunting once you're actually in your environment. And now you're struck with the reality of the limits of the resources you have to work with. It would be easy to wear yourself out during this time with random acts that consume enormous amounts of that precious spring energy, jumping from one idea or project to the next. Recognize that it is all a vital part of the spring energy—just don't try to do it all at once!

Creativity in Spring

Every business is creative, and as with most things creative, we reach a wall. Sometimes you can go for months or years without hitting it and sometimes, especially when you're at a transition, you hit it more often. The wall I'm talking about feels like exhaustion mingled with blankness, dread, confusion, and a good dose of doubt.

If you're a small business owner, you know what I'm talking about. It can feel as though you're drowning in a sea of unknowns, that you've left the familiar shores of safety and comfort behind you forever. This is only partly true. We are charting unfamiliar territory when we go into business, develop new services or products, or create new business relationships. This place can be quite disconcerting even if you've come through it time and time again. Maybe your safety zone is dealing with a certain type of client, or maybe it's doing everything yourself, or even the insistence on running a particular advertisement you've always had success with.

So how do you get past it, through it, over it—whatever? The first thing I coach my small business clients to do is to get out and meet other like-minded, spiritually uplifting people who thoroughly support you and understand you. This is important because in these uncharted waters, we sometimes lose sight of the fact that we are not alone. We are not islands—the best ideas are collaborative and connected in nature. Other people can be a great source of renewed energy for you. Sometimes the energy they give you is enough to give you the strength to either chip away at the wall or break through it.

Next, I tell my clients they need to visualize the outcome they are looking to evoke, to see the goal in all of its detail, fully alive and complete.

The last and most important thing is to take stock. This means to mentally give thanks for everything that *is* working for you right now, for everything you *have* accomplished up to this point. List at least ten things you've done successfully or that you're grateful for having in your life at this very moment.

Getting past the wall is a skill that we've got to master as entrepreneurs. But remember, it is just a wall and we can create around it, rise above it, or dig our way out from under it. However you manage to get past it, there is always something to be gained by meeting the wall.

Action

Generally, action, and lots of it, is what spring is all about; it literally launches us into the next phase of development. More specifically, this push takes the form of focusing on variations of these seven marketing questions:

• What do I do each day to attract new customers?

• What do I do each day to turn potential opportunities into actual business?

• What do I do to monitor my business everyday?

• What do I do to nurture the love factor in my customer relationships?

• How disciplined am I about my time?

• How do I build on my current knowledge and skills?

• How am I turning information into knowledge and that knowledge into wisdom for myself and for my customers?

Go ahead and take a stab at them. What you'll probably find is that you're spending more time on the things that *don't* produce the most income for your business. Things like overseeing every detail of the development of your brochure. Solution: take the extra time to find a good graphic designer and printer that you can develop a relationship with. Make sure to spend more time on clarifying and articulating your ideas and making sure you were understood and then let go, intervening only once in a while to monitor the development. Your time is invaluable at this stage in your business, so you can't be mismanaging such a precious resource on actions that don't produce the greatest returns for you.

In business, taking action often means presenting something to someone you've never met before, while trusting yourself and having confidence in the belief that a significant group of people somewhere would care enough to invest their money in what you have to offer. When it comes to taking action, knowing what you want out of it is a key factor. The objective could be to increase income, but that might just be a part of the story. Keep asking yourself before a meeting exactly what sort of outcome you want— exactly what your desire or intent is. Continue drilling down your every assumption until the objective is clear, precise, and achievable in as few steps as possible.

But what if it isn't the actions of a specific event that seems to be holding you back? What do you do if it's a fear of moving forward—the fear of more action—that seems to be immobilizing you? What then? It's important to know that behind every action is an emotion; now's the time to find out what lies behind your inaction.

Actions, Emotions, Procrastination, and the Big Picture

Emotions are what actually propel businesses forward. We use words like "motivation" and "passion," but what we're really talking about are emotions and in order to become better at managing the emotions of others, we need to become better managers of our own.

Becoming better managers of our emotions involves becoming conscious again, and that basically revolves around four subtle, yet conscious steps:

1. Identify the feeling or emotion.

2. Do something, one tiny thing, to maintain conscious movement, even if it is to stop and breathe for a while.

3. Find out how you really feel about success now.

4. Decide if you still want the goal.

We often run on automatic, especially with our feelings, and we fail to consider them as guideposts to a larger truth that is at the heart of the reality we have created.

When it comes to our emotions in business—frustration, fear, anxiety, greed—we rarely stop for a moment and consider what triggered them or what actions or events on a larger scale those emotions could then trigger. We need to become more conscious in business and realize that emotion is nothing more than energy in motion (e-motion). Emotions are never separate from our goals, our circumstances, our outcomes, or our actions even when the choice of action is inaction or the choice of emotional reaction is detachment.

Being an organic entrepreneur means being courageous enough to look at the various forms of emotions as they present themselves in our day-to-day business: fear, which can lead to procrastination or, worse, huge moral compromises; anger, which can lead to miscommunications; or lowered self-worth, which can lead to lowered sales. In essence, this is what we do as organic entrepreneurs: we turn potentially toxic substances (negative e-motions) into something nourishing and useful (positive e-motions). In business, as in most relationships, we typically are taught to focus on getting rid of "bad" emotions, but as organic entrepreneurs, we throw away as little as possible and reuse every experience for maximum benefits. The focus is on transformation. The trans-*formation* takes place in you the entrepreneur, your client, and your business. It draws your attention to the fact that sometimes even if the emotion is "bad," it could inherently be "good" if it leads to change, improvement, value, and wisdom for your environment.

Every aspect of your business dealings involves emotions, from prospecting to customer service, from sales and marketing to group collaborations. Through these, all that energy in motion is either expressed (in action) or repressed (creating a block in action).

Consider customer service. When your customers are "happy," they see your business as something "good." They want to align themselves to your business because they want to feel that good feeling again and again. And so they become repeat customers.

To be effective in business, we need to be sensitive to what others are feeling in any given situation. This requires empathy, the ability to understand another's situation, feelings, or motives. Before a business becomes truly conscious, its leaders and entrepreneurs typically say they "understand" a client's needs. But more often than not, this is only to pursue an end result (a sale) rather than it being based on a true desire to know.

How often as business owners, especially in the startup or small business phases, do we truly allow ourselves to feel or to empathize with our potential customers? But here is the real challenge: how many times do we do it *without* an ulterior motive? How often do we consider the emotional impact of our words upon our business environment?

If we want someone to take a particular action—such as purchasing our product—then it is important to not only consider but to also learn about the emotions that are driving that purchase because we don't ever act without first *feeling* something. Every action (or non-action) contains a feeling: if we are afraid, we may procrastinate or retreat into old habits, and if we are feeling anger, we unconsciously become impaired and destructive.

What many of us have been taught about the relationship between action and emotion is that first we need to *feel* a certain way before we *do* something. But in order to effectively move out of procrastination and many other unwanted states, the *doing* must precede the *feeling*. For example, if you want feel good about your sales efforts, you have to go out and knock on some doors. You will eventually get that sale or some feedback that buoys the confidence that drives you to continue. Many of us fall into the trap of waiting to be hit by inspiration or a good feeling, when all we need to do is simply perform an action to trigger the feeling we desire. Sometimes you're not going to like aspects of what you do, but at other times you're going to love it. You need to become a master at managing your emotions because they don't just affect you, they affect your entire environment as well.

When it comes to building positive business environments, the emotional climate is often overlooked, but we need to evaluate the triggers of an emotional climate within the structure we choose to create. These climates are usually created unconsciously from these and other triggers:

- our thoughts
- our beliefs and assumptions
- our networks
- our expectations
- our actions (including patterns or breaks in patterns)
- our words
- our customer and supplier interactions

In order to become masters of our emotions, it's important to evaluate the mood within your environment. Is it one you wish to continue to foster or should it be altered? As the entrepreneur-manager you are the guardian and overseer of your emotional environment, in addition to being the marketing, sales, and customer service departments. You must become vigilant at observing and accurately evaluating your own emotional state and that of your business and be able to wisely judge what's missing and what needs changing, such as positive, nourishing emotions that could replace toxic, negative ones.

One step in emotional mastery is paying attention to the emotional "charge" behind the words you use—not just with someone else, but first and foremost with yourself. Is your self-talk unsupportive or abusive? Is the "charge" of the words you use with others curt and cold, even though they seem like the right words? People are not fools; they get the real message behind the words even if you don't. The emotional environment needs to be right for your words to take hold and grow within a conversation. Even if you have the goal of a sale within a specific meeting, hold off making the pitch until a positive emotional environment has been created. Make a point of hiring people who can facilitate this consciously.

We can't talk about action without discussing procrastination. There is never a single reason why people put off doing things that are obviously necessary to reach the next step in their business journey. When it has become a head-scratcher that's when procrastination is likely about emotion. It isn't about the physicality of deadlines or pressures of performance but instead the nebulous, evasive churning that is so hard to get a handle on.

What typically stalls us is coming head-to-head with the enormity of something—our fear, an outdated belief, the size of a project, or the size of a dream. The way through this obstacle is to think small. Think mini. Break things down into the smallest pieces possible. Small can be accomplished with greater ease and current resources. All we need is a way—any way—to create a shift in how we look at a project that will get us over the wall and into to the next phase.

Think big, yes, but don't cram. One lead-up to procrastination is the planting of too many ideas at once and trying to do everything. Give your ideas room to breathe. Any small space (and a small business is a small space) that's full of "stuff" will inevitably look and feel cramped and cluttered. This can be suffocating and can potentially be taxing on your energy.

Be cautious with how many ideas you let loose in the beginning. Plant a few, give them your full attention, and as time goes by, in the wake of those that didn't make it, plant a few new ones. With each new planting, you'll grow keener in observation and will become familiar with those projects that are natural to your environment—that is your personality, character and lifestyle, outlook, and attitude. It's about trial and error, which is very action oriented.

Here are three things you can do quickly to support this shift in how you look at things, and by quick I mean under ten minutes a day. Do you think ten minutes a day is not enough to make a big difference? Think again: ten minutes a day equals adds up to approximately five hours a month! That's five hours of continually feeding your personal energy bank with positive currency! So use these three simple steps to move out of procrastination:

1) Become a visionary
Visualize the one miracle you hope to accomplish for the day (see it already completed). If it's the end of the day and you've already lived it, then relive it again in your mind's eye.

2) Be moved
Feel your body vibrate with the "charge" of happiness. If you're not happy now, then replicate a moment when you were.

3) Be the change you wish to see
Do one thing to support your goal today and every day! One act every day is 365 actions a year that support your dream, who you are, what you believe in, and not just someone else's agenda.

Let me tell you a secret: it's much easier to spare some time for small, conscious change and feel power-*full* than it is to deal with having it forced on you by your circumstances and feel power-*less*.

Designing Your Business

Since crafting a business is as much an art as it is a science, the art of designing the right business to suit your specific makeup takes trial and error. Spring is the time to set down your plans, the time to breathe the breath of life into your dreams and designs. Sure enough, this will bring them face to face with a reality that is either receptive or not—you never can tell until you begin to set them down.

Being an entrepreneur requires a definite degree of will. Some may argue that's all we have, but if over the winter of your business you were able to recognize and exert your will over the shaping of your character, then the use of your will over your design will not be as pronounced nor so tedious, rather it will be engaging and exciting. As you are designing the business, there are choices to be made about projects, suppliers, timing, cost, and priorities, and if you have a family, then their concerns and opinions also need to be a factor in the design process.

You may choose to either wind your way casually toward a symbiotic system or create it more synthetically by hiring consultants and expert advisers right away. You can source the most inexpensive hardware, software, and equipment for your business, which would save you money for other operating costs, or you can buy the best right off the bat and pick your way through your budget for the rest of the fiscal year—or find a way in between. However you choose to approach your business in spring, I will share with you what I have learned about designing a business—the resources, the fiscal factors, your environment and community, and the impact they all have on the ongoing design of your enterprise.

Respect

One thing we need to learn to do is respect the "soil" out of which our business grows, the soil out of which you with your dreams, desires, and needs spring forth and are fed. The soil is your essence and your environment; it is that sacred place within you that connects your life to the lives of your clients, suppliers, staff, and investors. It is where you go at the beginning of your search for a way to serve and be served through business. It's also where you go when you feel you've finished contributing in this way, when you're ready to plan your exit strategy. As an organic entrepreneur, your soil is where you go to heal and restore your self during the various ups and downs. Without a healthy respect for your soil, there can be no community, only greed and selfishness—there would be no soul to your business.

Money and Meaning

Merging profit with purpose is the challenge of our times, and it begins within the heart of each entrepreneur. How do we deal with money, how can we better negotiate money, how do we interact and relate to lots of it or not enough of it? How much is enough to make us feel happy or accomplished? All good questions; some we can answer here, but many more you need to search and shine the light on for yourself and realize that it will never truly be enough. This fact is not a bad thing, however, because we will come to realize that once our needs are satisfied, only so much can be fed from the confines of money. This is why we factor in meaning—beyond money, there is only meaning. This wanting more doesn't in and of itself make you greedy, it just means you're evolving, changing beyond the dictates of your present circumstances. You've outgrown your pot, now you need the earth.

If ever there were an extremely emotional and volatile subject, money is it. So where do we begin with such an emotional subject as this? Start by becoming clear, crystal clear about what is enough for you. How much do you need to make you authentically happy to the bones? I think it's really important to ask yourself this question before you attempt to jump-start your business. If you already have a business, take the time now to discover and articulate this for yourself. How do you define success? Why is having more money even important to you? Why are you choosing to do it through self-employment; why don't you just find a good job? If you don't ask yourself these vital questions about money, how else will you know you've reached your goals if you haven't a clue what the landscape at the destination should look like or feel like? How much money is enough in exchange for your time? How much personal time or time away from your family is too much? How much travel, use of your creativity, how much "stuff" is enough to make you happy being an entrepreneur?

This book began with the suggestion of discontentment. If this is your current reality, then what are you discontented about and how does it need to be different for you to feel like you're engaged with meaning? What qualities do you need to see expressed in your day for it to become worthwhile? One crucial question that people rarely ask themselves at the beginning of the journey is, "Could I foresee money changing me? If so, in what way?" If you say money won't change you, you're definitely not being honest with yourself. It's like saying that having an extra 100 watts of energy surge through your body wouldn't change your physical make up. Sure it would!

Money is energy, it is *currency,* and you will be changed by its influx into your life. The intelligent approach would be to get to know yourself better so you can manage your reactions to making money and minimize the risk of becoming a victim of the surge. You will have greater control if you decide *now* how you choose to balance such an eventuality. Money makes you grow up very quickly; are you prepared to grow up now if financial success were to happen quicker than you expected?

These questions should be prerequisites to starting a business and it boggles my mind that more banks don't do a better job at helping people become more financially fluent. Becoming fluent in finance is essential to the organic entrepreneur because money is a language and it's a language we use to communicate effectively with all aspects of our environment. If you're not yet comfortable with speaking the language of money, you'd better learn how to be—and fast. It's not only important for you but also for your customers. If you can translate what you do for them into savings or earnings, you've become a much greater asset to their lives.

Learning the language of money and finance means you won't be put off or intimidated by the important details of cash flow and balance sheets; it means you'll be able to ask critical, informed questions such as: when is the business profitable or at what point will the business break even? How much do I need to have to be somewhat stress free if the business doesn't make money right away? Not knowing how to speak this language makes an entrepreneur feel like a financial cripple. Sure you can function, but you don't have full access to all of your potential.

Be clear about what you can afford to lend to the business and how long you might have to wait before you can see a return, and accept the probability that you might never see it back again. Can you afford to wait comfortably for two, three, or even five years before your business can give back to you? If you can't, then your map needs to be modified to include a part-time job or a reduction in expenses.

Money and Creativity

Spring is also a time when your business runs the risk of being flooded with too much too soon. Is this a problem you think you'd like to have? Probably not right away. Think about it, we all want and need water for life but if it starts pouring in from your roof, your basement, your windows, and your leaky faucets, then that resource can easily become a nightmare. Pretty soon all you're thinking about are the leaks and nothing else! The same example can be applied to money and it's potential effects on creativity. And, yes, while no business can survive without its fair share of money, too much of it can prove much more harmful than helpful because without mastery over money it tends to suffocate organic growth and creativity.

When it comes to your business, how much you charge for your product or service is key. If you can't charge more for a service either because of leaner economic times or because you've hit a price ceiling, what then? How can you still profit without raising prices? Finding the answer to this for your business is creativity at work. Mastering the language of money in your life, whether it be for your personal or business life, comes through four phases:

Disbelief

It's a numb feeling. You're locked in a holding pattern that seems to never change. Whether it's continuous purchasing without a real need or the refusal to see that you have more than an unhealthy stack of outstanding, unpaid invoices while you continue to service the same clients.

Distress

This leads to sleeplessness over money—the constant worry and tension where the mere thought of money brings a highly uncomfortable physical reaction.

Acceptance

Here, the courage and the strength is gathered that allows you to see the truth of the current situation and accept it for exactly what it is. This helps you realize that these are only unhealthy *choices* and that this has no reflection on your worth or value as a human being, just your choice of actions.

Consciousness

This last phase of money mastery involves becoming aware, no matter how variably, of all of the times you've agreed to use your power to manifest a certain reality based on your current beliefs and mobilizing all your intentions and resources to act with integrity and wholeness now.

Money and Fear

Debt, whether it manifests in your personal or your business life, is a silent, isolating disease that cripples millions of people every day all over the world. When you own a business, you can buy anti-suppressants for your fears in the form of hiring people to do the things you fear doing the most, such as hiring an accountant or a salesperson. The solutions you buy, however, are not as resilient as the ones you cultivate by mastering or even attempting to master your money fears and rising above their grip. One of the greatest fears that we have in business apart from dealing with the details of money is the fear of negotiating, which involves the anticipation of money and is supercharged with emotion.

Negotiating is the art of monetizing value by understanding the perceptions experienced through communication. When it comes to negotiating, it's the fear of *not* getting what we want—the fear of not making an income, the fear of losing, the fear of getting less than what we think we're worth—that blocks us and lands us with much less than what we desired or envisioned. Nowhere else do our beliefs and fears around money become more alive, more clear, than when we are about to negotiate for more money. Mastering the art of negotiation and the subsequent fear that arises as a result takes knowing yourself, focusing your attention, and rallying your energies in the following ways:

1. Know your values and negotiate from the one that speaks the loudest at that time. Is it the value of autonomy, creativity, or travel that motivates you now? Whatever it is, acknowledge that value and know that you're acting to satisfy it.

2. Manage your fear, don't try to obliterate it. This is not a seek-and-destroy mission. If you attempt to destroy it, it will only change its form and lull you into a false sense of safety only to crop up somewhere else. The plain truth is that we will never rid ourselves of fear; we've just got to become masters at managing it and not the other way around. Find a healthy method to minimize its effects, such as yoga, conscious breathing, meditation, or walking.

3. Tell yourself the truth. Acknowledge the outcome that you fear the most. If you have a fear of going back to a 9 to 5, then unmask it and bring it out into the open. Simply say out loud, "I am afraid of having to go back to work for someone else, I think it would mean the death sentence of my soul." There. It's out. At least now you won't have it lurking around the corners scaring the wits out of you when you're the most unsuspecting. You've reduced the charge it has on you and now you can use some of that energy you've been using to keep the truth of what you fear at bay to inspire solutions instead.

4. Hold your vision clearly and consistently. In negotiations, it's the vision of whoever has the power to leave the strongest impression that gets realized. A weak, wishy-washy vision of your outcome will never have the power to impress itself upon reality. Your vision needs to be clearer and more charged than your fears. Period.

5. Figure out what "more money" is trying to say. Is it really about the need for more recognition, more creative influence, greater access to influential connectors? Figure out what the pursuit of more means to you at the moment of negotiations and you'll be clearer and you'll know if you have it, even if the contract doesn't look exactly like what you itemized point for point.

6. Know thyself. It is critical, once and for all, as individuals and business owners, that we rid ourselves of the belief that an amount of money reflects our self-worth or value as a human being. If you are starting a business from this premise, your foundation will always be shaky and you will run the risk of losing perspective during negotiations and losing opportunities because you lack the ability to be truly objective.

7. Do the due diligence. Research, research, research! The more you know about all the facets of the business and people with whom you'll be negotiating, the better you will know the terrain. Research things such as their track record, what motivates them or would make them want to take the deal, and also the industry standards for the amount that you're proposing.

If you consider these seven elements, negotiating takes on a different appearance because suddenly fear and money are both put into their proper perspective and they've been consciously factored into your equation.

Money and Power

The quest to make more money, to make a successful living for ourselves, is only a tool to stretch, test, polish, and further develop our characters so we begin living more like the great entities we truly are—so we can begin working with a cleaner, more refined energy. The continued commitment to make and attract money, this self-realization through self-employment, can drag up the worst demons, and, yet, through it all, money only serves as a magnifier of our present state of acceptance revealing all of our assumptions about how we believe the world works and our true net "worth."

We would sooner produce 25 cents to give to a homeless person than spend 25 minutes working on changing our mental money moulds (i.e., the way we perceive whealth and the elements that block us from having a continuous flow of cash.) This made me ask these questions early on: how much personal change have I made room for to attract more opportunities for whealth? How much space have I given to accommodate a new way of thinking and being that is consistent with whealth? Early on, the answer was...not *nearly* enough.

If there is no room in your mind for a mental shift in perspective around money, then how can you ever expect your body, and ultimately your life, to make room for more? The actions that dictate the body's movement take their cue from your thoughts on a moment-by-moment basis, so this shift is crucial. Make the time to consciously drive the changes that support your dreams and your plans for whealth: the success of your business depends upon it.

Principles of Organic Marketing

In business, just about everything comes down to marketing and so we do our very best to try to understand how it works specifically for *our* business. Marketing is how we communicate our value to our markets—it's how we say we're here, we're alive, and we're ready to serve. Marketing is what we use to maintain momentum after the initial kick off. And while many will tell you of all the tangible benefits of marketing, I'm going to introduce you to some principles of *great* marketing that few business courses even talk about.

What if you were to consider just for a moment that we are spirits living human experiences rather than the more widely accepted notion that we are humans sometimes experiencing but most often seeking spiritual experiences? It would change the way you looked at every aspect of your life, wouldn't it? It would even change the way you looked and acted in business. It's by asking this question again and again that I've come to the awareness of these principles in marketing.

Marketing pushes our ideas out into the open; through it, we end up exposed, out on a limb, and risking our comfortable place to communicate and build a community around an idea (there's more about communication and community later in the chapter on autumn). That's what we're here for—the experience, not to be perfect. These seven organic marketing principles below are simply a guide to help you build a more conscious marketing map from the start, a map that is more in line with who you are.

Consciousness

In business today *unconsciousness* is the centerpiece of profit. And yet, despite this, these are exciting times in the world of enterprise. Right now there is an evolution toward consciousness happening in business, albeit slowly, and it's turning business into a great place for entrepreneurs like ourselves who know in our bones that there is a way to merge profit with purpose. This movement is *con-*

scious because business is becoming aware of itself and *evolving* because the process of positive change is unfolding like a flower to take the vehicle of business to a higher state of co-creation with everything it touches.

Up until now, people in business have used the structure of a corporation, which is a separate and distinct entity, to separate and convince themselves, as though they were schizophrenics, that they are not the ones who are perpetrating the grievous act of putting profit before people, endangering the very souls of those who work for them, those who provide them with their income, as well as the planet. Don't get me wrong, I'm not advocating putting people before profit either. This would just be more of the same only from a different end of the spectrum. As organic entrepreneurs, we are through with excessives and extremes—what we crave is *balance* through consciousness.

What I'm drawing your attention to here is the development of greater self-recognition of what we choose to grow or manifest in the "soil" and how each action, no matter how small, has an equal and opposite reaction throughout the world. Sometimes it's as close to home as your employees or your investors, and other times it can affect someone halfway around the world. Without consciousness, we are without a soul. Consciousness in business is more easily injected into small- to medium-sized corporations, where the effects can be almost immediate. In bigger businesses, the ripple effect can be so slow as to seem non-existent and so most of us would lose hope and the energy to continue, but it *can* be done.

At the centre of the conscious business is conscious thought since thought always appears before the action. So in order to allow for a different consciousness in business, we must allow room for and facilitate alternative ways of thinking within the individual. And as we evolve to this new consciousness in business, we are recognizing that we will need to adopt different business skills, especially in marketing, and a lot of these tools will come as a result of the continued development of ourselves into fully conscious human beings.

A world full of conscious businesses can only exist if we, as individuals, have the strength and courage to maintain our individual self-consciousness. It is then that we can awaken to the possibility, and subsequent reality, of businesses being self-conscious and responsible entities answering to more than just their fiscal imperatives.

Love

About this word, in all of our existence, we have said everything and nothing at all. There is more. That's because love is an experience. It has to be experienced and shared to know it intimately, to then be able to go out and communicate it. So if love is mainly an experience and marketing and branding is about "the experience," then why do we resist working with love through conscious application in our business relationships? This just doesn't seem sensible.

The next level in business relationships without a doubt is about getting to love. The next generation of marketing is about how to get customers to love you and your product or service to make them passionate advocates of your brand. When we love something, we hold nothing back; we see more of the good, and when there is love, there is more tolerance and understanding during rough times. For this reason, love is good for business and it generates repeat business. Reasoning can compare, add, and subtract, but it isn't what ultimately pushes customers beyond digging into their wallets and paying for your product to establishing a long-term relationship of reverence.

If we love what we do, then we shouldn't be ashamed to market with love, speak about our product with love, and create loving bonds with each and every prospect or client that comes in contact with us personally or our brand.

Attraction

Attraction = Love in Action. When there is greater attraction, marketing is much more effortless a practice. There really are two parts to attraction: love and action. If you're not attracting enough business, typically there is a disconnect between one or the other. Either the flow of love for your business is blocked or there isn't enough action to support the love. Some things that could be blocking the love or action are: worry and doubt, fear, confusion, or being overwhelmed.

The thing to do to realign yourself with attraction again is to get honest about the present moment—what's really going on, what is the real (not perceived) danger, if any? Next, be clear about where you want your thoughts, feelings, and actions to be directed because we all know that what we focus on is what gets fed or magnified.

Now that you know this, there is a very simple and easy way to make money in your business and that is to become highly attractive. When we're making a sale, we're thinking of the end result, of the money we'll be making, instead of being in love with the benefits your service or product will bring to the life of the human being in front of you. You will always have to close the sale, either by signing a contract or by swiping a credit card. This part never goes away. But when it's motivated by love, it's organic, authentic; it becomes as engaging and unencumbered as asking someone out that you know darn well likes you. Think iPod and the millions of buyers it has attracted. Apple doesn't need to make sales pitches because they've got millions of people reaching into their pockets to give them money because Apple gives their customers something they love. They're giving them mobile entertainment: music, movies, and information they love—that's love in action When people can visualize themselves engaged with joy in your product or service, that's love in action, that's attraction, and it's effortless because the customer is visualizing with feeling and making the sale on their own.

Integrity

Corporate integrity begins and ends with the integrity of self—*all* of the self: physical, emotional, mental, and spiritual. We have been taught in our school systems and our jobs that we can function if only two parts of the human being are present, namely the physical and mental parts. The parts that drag us out of bed, drive us to work, punch-in for eight hours a day, and cash the paycheque. This message has always been clear in business—just don't bring your emotional and spiritual parts or you could find yourself not included in meetings, not getting promoted, or worse, out of a job.

What we've been doing up until now is breeding two-dimensional people with little depth or insight in a multi-dimensional, complex environment and we're surprised at the results! If you stop for a moment, you'll notice that a lack of integrity gradually builds from too much internal "noise"—expert opinions, assumptions, figures—which causes a sort of spiritual dissonance or discord that before long drowns out the voice of your true values. It almost never happens all at once; it's always gradual with little concessions made here and there that slowly erode the soul or miniscule pieces of yourself sold for a trinket or a bauble. We eventually learn there's never enough to feed the soul, the whole person.

Maintaining personal and business integrity takes maintaining a sort of constant inner communion. In order to understand the many problems we have had so far with integrity, we need to look at our problems with the truth. What's so wrong with the truth, your truth, world truth? If we're afraid of the truth that our product sucks and no one will buy it, then, yes, we run the risk of sinking good money into misdirected advertising. If we're afraid to hear that the sales team is losing sales because they don't understand the product, the message, or, worse, don't believe in it, then we can never get to a true solution, every subsequent effort will only be a band-aid.

Are we on integrity 100% of the time? Probably not. But does this mean then that we shouldn't even try or shouldn't hold ourselves accountable if we veer off the path of integrity? No. Integrity should always be sought after, measured, and encouraged just like the P&L statements, especially in the forum of business, where the choice of one has a domino effect for so many others. Knowing this, I would darn well want my bosses to be on integrity and personal values since their choices affect my life, the lives of my children and my partner, my thoughts, my moods, my choices. These are just some of the far-reaching effects of integrity and you can see we've only begun to scratch the surface.

Influence

I introduced integrity first because in order to affect events, people, or things without any direct or apparent effort (the definition of influence), we need to have personal power and we can't have personal power without integrity. When you're in business, you're not just in the media business or the banking business or the clothing business, you're also in the influence business.

Many organic entrepreneurs often shy away from influence and personal power because we have all witnessed too many cases over the years where the two have become so perverted with self-interest that it almost always appears one-sided and never shared: we think we have to turn our backs on them if we are to build a conscious business. But we cannot be effective if our business is lacking in influence or personal power. To understand the source of influence, we must let go and accept that there is indeed the mysterious and the unknown. To some extent, we can control it, but largely, the power of influence rests in a willingness to be guided by this mysterious and unknown, to let that energy of influence flow through you. But not many of us want to let anything in, we want to affect the world without being changed by it, but by the nature of the word *influence*, this is impossible.

The word *influence* comes from the Latin *in-fluere* meaning "in-flow" or a flowing into *us*. If we can work in conscious union with this power, then we can accomplish much more. Business is only one medium of influence but it is an important medium because it empowers our Source of energy to flow through us and touch other lives. Influence has to do with personal energy and we'll be exploring that later in this chapter. Much of our personal power and ability to influence lies untapped in part due to a lack of understanding of this energy but mainly because of a fear of what would happen if we allowed the energy of life to flow freely through us. And so our natural ability to build great businesses remains untapped, well below the surface of the commonplace.

If we think that businesses such as Microsoft and The Body Shop are large businesses that do much good in the world, imagine what could actually be accomplished if we were *consciously* working with this power for a greater good? Where we get mixed up is in the belief that power is equal to influence, but this couldn't be more wrong.

We think we have to force our way through a problem or to a solution with others (mainly to get them to see things our way), but influence works differently. Power is more external and raw, whereas influence is more internal and subtle emanating outward from within. The ability to consciously influence our environment, positively and ethically, is not just an important leadership quality, it is a vital life skill.

Failure

Failure is the compost of your business. Failure occurs more often than success when we are learning and growing, and yet most of us try to put as much distance as we can between failure and ourselves when it does happen. We try to throw it into the deepest, darkest pit, never to be seen or heard from again. Herein lies the answer to this struggle: failure is not the problem; our *reaction* to failure is.

Failure is natural. This is why earlier I said it's important to try small projects because the failures are then smaller and more acceptable. Furthermore, you can assimilate these failures into your environment more quickly so you can get familiar with your reactions to them and reduce the fear factor. This way, they don't overwhelm you or your business and you can learn from them in bits.

Nothing is ever a waste in creation; everything gets recycled—even ideas—because what constitutes a failure today could just be an idea that hasn't yet found its time for tomorrow. What's a failure now is just another opportunity to explore, another aspect of your ability to co-create with something greater.

I remember one of my first business failures. My partner and I were way ahead of the Internet curve in Canada, so we were coming up against many roadblocks in launching one of the first retail sites, but it just so happened that one of the suppliers we were courting for our website business asked us to be the general managers of a new flagship store being planned for Toronto. We couldn't have planned for nor imagined a more perfect opportunity—before our business plans—and if we wanted it, it was ours for the taking. This was one great opportunity that came out of a "failure" to find financing and get a great idea off the ground.

Failure is not the enemy; it is our unexpected fertilizer. If you look closely at the word *fertilizer*, you'll find nestled in there comfortably the world *fertile*. In biological terms, it means "capable of initiating, sustaining, or supporting reproduction." At the nucleus of failure rests the very same possibility: to support, sustain, and inspire new ideas that actually *do* work.

If your goal, then, as organic entrepreneurs is to build conscious businesses that serve more than just your own needs, wants, and desires, then you need to evolve to a point where you are more than just comfortable with failure, you need to revel in it as much as you revel in your successes. Failure takes us to the edge and that is a very uncomfortable place to be. If you are testing in small doses, you're probably also failing in small doses too, so plan for failure.

Realize as well that many of us may also be pulling out some great ideas that people have never even thought of or seen before. But that's a price that very few people are willing to pay, being so close to failure. Failure exposes our shame. Failure lays us bare. We have to overcome our aversion to failure if we are to thrive in our own soil. How much is your business inventing and testing in small amounts, in prototyping ideas? How much do you factor in your budget for failed attempts?

Becoming comfortable with failure takes a new kind of awareness and sensitivity—it takes intuition. These are not exactly words that inspire investors to dump loads of cash into a fledgling business, nor are they what board members are looking for in CEOs.

Everyone wants to work in the realm of possibilities, of what is known, of what already exists and as far away from the impossible as they can get—that place where amazing services and products live, because it's where doubt, failure, and uncertainty live too. Yet, we access this place when we first start out in business only to hold onto our first success and ride it into the sunset, never risking failure ever again and always going for safety and certainty—as far away from failure as possible.

One thing that would be quite innovative and that could lead us to healthier business models would be to embrace failure by planning for it—at least a couple of failures a year. They don't have to be big, but they should be included in the marketing and design plans of your business. The key is to gather every single piece of information gleaned from your failures so you can synthesize them. It's important when risking and experimenting with your approaches in business to be authentic and remain true to the values of your business. Then, there will never be a sense of loss.

As human beings, we should remind ourselves that we are always experimenting, meaning our experiments and creations can sometimes be failures. They sometimes don't achieve the desired end, but what if they achieve something much greater than our initial dream? This is something that could make you a lot of money, which is worth a failure or two.

Agreement

There can be no economy without agreement, and business cannot exist without it either. Where there is agreement, there is a sale. But let's look a bit further. Where there is agreement there is harmony, integrity, and a union of values, beliefs, and vision. In business, it is essential that others agree or are in harmony with your concepts, ideas, services, and products. When you find that agreement, it's almost like finding the key to a treasure box greater than anything the two of you could have ever discovered alone—client and creator. Think us and our BlackBerries, think us and our computers, think us and our books, us and the cooking channel, us and massage therapy—heck, us and any product that improves our lives for that matter! The sum of the union must be greater than the parts (i.e. the client's needs and our product or service). The place where agreement to purchase lives is that place where your values, vision, empowerment, and beliefs meet with those of your clients or prospects.

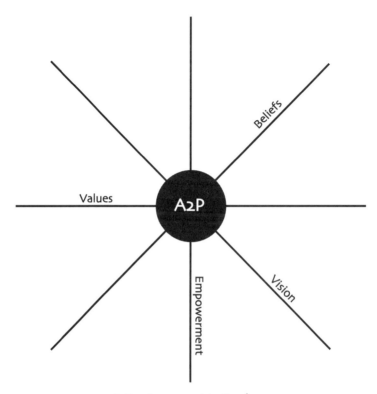

A2P = Agreement to Purchase

Nothing happens until there is agreement. Ad agencies working on behalf of their clients spend millions of dollars to create agreements between us and their clients because they know that before you make a purchase, there must be an agreement, and before you can get someone's agreement, you need to get their attention. I've said it before in *The Naked Millionare* and I'll say it again, it is *attention*, not money, that is the currency of this new economy.

To better understand this, it's important to look at the process of business as continuous exchanges of energy: attention (energy of focused awareness or consciousness), agreement (energy of unity and integrity), and sale (energy of money or currency). At the centre of it all is you—you the generator and manager of a mass of energy in the form of ideas, visions, passion, knowledge, wisdom, skills, etc. If any one of these are missing or out of alignment within you, money, integrity, or consciousness, then this piece of the marketing puzzle—the agreement—happens inconsistently, poorly, not at all, or has disastrous effects.

When you have someone's attention, you have more than just an opportunity to create an agreement that could lead to a sale, you have the opportunity to create a positive shift within someone's life. Now ask yourself this: what would the world be like if there was little conscious awareness of these energy dynamics and their consequences? The answer: exactly what we see now in business today. We, as buyers and citizens of this planet, are misguided in our belief that it is money that makes the world go around, and in being so misguided we give away our most valuable currency (attention) without a second thought. When we do and it is not returned with equal value, we feel duped, cheated, and drained, and a part of us becomes cynical.

We have an obligation as organic entrepreneurs to make sure that this energy exchange is clean and remains just that: an exchange of equally valuable energy resources. One is not more valuable than the other and each, attention and product or service must be respected.

The Benefits of Basic Needs

We as human beings have basic needs that will likely never change. According to Maslow's theory, there is actually a hierarchy of five levels of basic needs. They are:

1. *Physiological* – (i.e. food, water, oxygen, and warmth) These include the most critical needs and they must be met for biological survival;

2. Safety – To feel secure and out of danger. For example: knowing you have enough to pay your bills can make you feel safe;

3. Love – To have a sense of belonging, be accepted, and feel in community with others. When we sign up for forums with other like-minded people, we are seeking love;

4. Self-esteem – Success, to achieve desired goals, to have recognition and approval;

5. Self-realization – Finding self-fulfillment and realizing our own personal potential.

We become more effective marketers when we can align our products and services with one or more of these basic needs. As I examine marketing strategies and advertising spreads, there is often a common thread: the benefits of a product or service are closely aligned to at least one of these five basic needs. For example, the Nike ad "Just Do It" is speaking to our need for self-realization, as is the Adidas ad "Impossible Is Nothing." There is an ad for the Insurance Brokers Association of Canada where people are wrapped in blankets; the benefit they seek to communicate resonates with our need to feel safe and secure. It's important to know what these basic needs are so your marketing efforts can land with impact among your audience and give them what they need.

First, find out what the primary need motivating your audience is. We all move in and out of any of these needs at various times in our lives, but we generally relate to one more deeply than the others. Even if we have water freely flowing to wash our clothes, we still need pure drinking water, as pure as we can get. Even if the oxygen we breathe is life-sustaining, if we suffer from a lung problem, then our desire or need for cleaner air in our homes and where we live, work, and play increases greatly. These examples illustrate someone whose basic need is still physiological in nature. So these needs may be met on some level, but we can and will always want more and better—it is just evolution. Find out what need your product or service satisfies in your ideal client and build your marketing strategy around communicating that need powerfully and clearly.

Most self-starters are motivated by self-actualization and that's no different for you or me in business. It's the number one need driving me. But I've discovered the secondary need for me is also a very powerful need for most people: the need to feel safe and secure. Even though most people see self-employment as very risky business and entrepreneurs as risk takers, what most of us are after is security, although this might seem like an oxymoron.

For me, running my own business means safety and security because I've been fired and laid off from more jobs than I have fingers to count them and as a single mother with the responsibility of raising a child, I never could feel a sense of continuity or safety in a 9 to 5. With running my own business, safety comes from knowing that my tomorrow depends on my actions, thoughts, and feelings *today*. I was sure to structure my business so that what I get back has a more balanced relationship with what I put out there than if I worked for someone else.

Now how does this basic need line up with the benefit of my business? My business is aimed at people who are ready to stretch beyond the ordinary, people who are ready to create and express their dreams in ways they never have before. My business aims to satisfy the need of self-realization in others.

If you want to create greater impact with less effort, then try aligning your benefits with a basic need and you'll be surprised at the impact your marketing efforts create.

Southern Exposure

I overheard a conversation in a public washroom. I hung around, unseen, to hear what they'd say and how the two women would deal with their dilemma. They were students preparing to construct their graphics portfolio and they needed to have content describing their pieces, mainly about themselves. It seemed to be a requirement of the course. The one bemoaned that it was next to torture to have to populate the page with interesting and salesworthy tidbits about who she was and why anyone should hire her. The other commiserated, saying she felt the same way, that she found it easier to find great things to write about other people, but when it came to herself she was at a loss and that most everyone she spoke to felt the same way.

Upon emerging from my hiding spot, I contemplated why we find it so hard to sell ourselves? Why do we, especially women, find it hard to put ourselves out there when it comes to business?

What scares us about marketing is being exposed. I think that's mainly it—putting ourselves out there. This is what marketing feels like to most people: being up on a precipice with our tail flapping in the wind—most unbecoming and most vulnerable.

Marketing comes down to having the courage to acknowledge your own value, the willingness to connect with a larger audience through the media, and influencing others. Yes, there are a heap of other things we would rather be doing than be so achingly *visible* while asking for a sale. We keep thinking that there *must* be another way to get people to know who we are and that we are good—good enough to open the wallet for. Let me think for a moment…*no, there isn't.* There really is no other way for people to know how great you are and how worthy of their money your creativity, skills, and expertise are unless you package all of that value into something that has perceived value for someone else. It's vital to the survival of your business that you open up and expose yourself to the elements within your environment, to passionately embrace marketing.

For some of us, this is not our nature. I live in a culture where we seem to passionately *avoid* exposing ourselves in any way, including marketing, at all cost. Some of us may have been brought up in a culture that believes if you absolutely must engage in marketing and accolades do get heaped upon you, it's best to pretend it happened quite by accident and that you didn't really mean to become so successful at what you do. So for all you shy people out there, I understand. But at the same time, I am compelled to urge you, to plead with you to put as much energy and passion into promoting and displaying your best assets to your market, the media, the world, and anyone else who will listen to you. If you've put the time, money, and effort into starting a company, it is vital that you be prepared for the task of good, strong, passionate marketing.

Why the Shame in Marketing?

The battles of self-promotion and marketing for an entrepreneur are mainly fought on an internal battlefield. Many great products or services never see the light of day because of this fear of self-promotion, which is loosely connected to shame. I was out on a book tour and it was while speaking to the manager of a bookstore that a light bulb went on for me. He said to me, "You've got to be a shameless marketer to be a successful author." All the while, I was thinking why have shame at all? Since when did that word elbow its way into any relationship with marketing?

Marketing oneself is an art and for many, including myself in the beginning, it takes courage to embrace it fully. For many entrepreneurs, self-promotion is a continuous struggle. I read an article in the newspaper recently about a veteran Stratford theatre actor who suffered from a near-crippling fear of performing in public for eighteen years! Self-promotion can often seem like performing in public and it can be a scary place if we lose sight of the fact that it is born out of love for what we do and the desire to share it with as many people as we can in this world. Where is the shame in love and sharing if it includes profit?

Where is the shame in standing on the rooftops and telling everyone you know of that you have an amazing product or service that could improve their lives? Where is the shame in calling up the media and letting them know that you have news that could make their audiences happier, wealthier, sexier, more peaceful, or whatever?

There is no shame in authentic value. There is no shame in self-promotion. As an entrepreneur, small business owner, author, or artist, you are doing yourself a serious injustice and continually blocking the message when you introduce shame with marketing or self-promotion. I choose to use the term "vigorous" self-promotion, meaning strong, energetic, and active in mind or body. What this means is that we cannot approach marketing or self-promotion in a half-hearted way or that is what we will get: a half-hearted response.

For me, the problem had always been *continuous* self-promotion. I would never talk about the cool things I had accomplished or could do for clients outside of a seminar, workshop, or my writing (and even that sometimes was painful). I remember when people would come up to me and compliment me on my writing or my ability with foreign languages at functions and I'd brush it off as coincidental. It wasn't false modesty, it was a block—it was the shame of talking too much about myself and the feeling that drawing too much attention to myself would bring negative scrutiny, which would hurt. Now I acknowledge these inferior emotions and challenge myself anyway to step out and speak as many times as I can and as vigorously as I can about the benefits of what I bring to the world.

There is no place for false pride or self-effacing behaviour when you're speaking to the media or your market about the virtues of your product or service. If you have something to say that could help the world, then for goodness sake, speak up! We can all use something good in our lives. The only shame in marketing is doing a lukewarm job of it.

Owning Your Craft

Another aspect of marketing is the way we present ourselves to the world in what we wear and how we act. Dressing for success has a lot more to do with owning your own space than it does with what you actually wear. We've all heard that it's important to dress the part if you want the part: shoes well polished, suit freshly laundered, a nice clean haircut, etc. But have you ever stopped to consider that it has very little to do with the clothes, that it could have something to do with an element that is a lot more elusive than your sartorial choices? No one's ever told us that in order to be successful we can't just occupy space, we've got to own it. That's what a television producer and coach of mine told me when I hired her to help me get to the next level in my relationship with the media.

The first thing "Jennifer" (not her real name) brought to my attention was that I was not owning my space: in fact, I was retreating or hiding within very nice clothes. Here's what happened: I was lucky enough to find myself in a meeting with three executives from a production company that made shows for a major network. They needed someone for a new show they wanted to pitch to the network and my coach had suggested I interview for it.

I was both thrilled and intimidated, but at least I had

fashion savvy and could wow them with the brilliance of my clothes and how I wore them...or so I thought. I ended up wearing a beautiful deep purple shawl and a nice suit underneath it. It was winter and I was nervous, and when I get nervous, I sweat. The sweat made me very cold and I ended up wrapping myself in my shawl throughout most of the interview. It came as no surprise that they didn't choose me as the host of the pilot.

When I spoke to Jennifer later that week, she told me that I didn't own my space. I didn't understand what she was getting at, not fully. She explained that I appeared to be hiding in the shawl, that it seemed I was getting smaller and smaller in what I was wearing! I couldn't believe it, but it was true. When I looked back on the interview, I had done everything right. I wore the right clothes and said the right things, but something was off—I did shrink into a very tiny space. I tried to take up as little space as possible because I felt dwarfed by the opportunity. I didn't own the space I was taking up.

Being successful at what you do means claiming every aspect of the space you occupy and never shrinking from the weight, the attention, the accolades, or the moral obligations that come with such success. Being a successful entrepreneur means moving out of a spiritual and mental "rental" space and taking ownership of the space you have chosen to live in, no matter what your craft. Being successful is a responsibility that many shrink from thereby making it even more elusive because when you desire something and are unable to grasp it, you simply end up wishing and hoping.

If Wishes Were Horses

An acquaintance of mine recently bought a business. It was a small landscaping business that had built up a good reputation but was still in its infancy. He wanted to take it to the next level and expected to turn a very healthy profit immediately upon purchase. Unfortunately, he forgot that a business is about relationships and that he, now the new owner, needed to establish a new bond with the current client base even though they were already great customers of the previous owner. He had great expectations, but the truth is that great expectations typically rest upon very shaky business ground.

After only six months, I heard he was now selling the business and wanted out. He said he didn't want to risk losing any more money and didn't like how it consumed his family life. These are valid reasons for getting out, but ones that clearly illustrate that not everyone is cut out to be an entrepreneur, a realization that is totally okay. It's better to come to that realization sooner rather than later.

But where was the initial research or the soul searching he'd done to see if this venture was a good fit or whether it would meet, in any shape or form, his expectations? What was interesting was whether he was in it for the love of landscaping or for the love of money. He quite openly admitted that he was only in it for the profits (sorry, potential profits) that he saw while the previous owner had it. But he wasn't coming at it from the heart and would never be satisfied with any decent amount he made in the beginning. Had he put more of his energy into building a successful business instead of *wishing* he had one, he might have been able to make something wonderful from an already good business.

Spring isn't about wishing, spring is about action. If you're not ready for action—lots of it—then it might get too hot for you. When you find yourself doing more wishing than acting, it could be a sign.

Too many great businesses are flushed down the tubes because the would-be entrepreneur admits too late that what they really wanted was to fulfill a wish, not live a dream. There's nothing wrong with wanting a wish fulfilled; they are actually granted every once in a while, believe it or not, but you can't build a business on them. Marketing takes action, not wishes.

When we're not willing to do the work, commit the time, or make the necessary inner adjustments for our business to grow, but still expect success, we are like beggars with both hands forever outstretched—one begging for a free meal ticket and the other thumbing for a free ride. If we are to grow a business organically, then no matter how successful we become at our craft, our hands should always be deep in the dirt with the watering can beside us, rather than praying for rain.

When Opportunity Knocks, Do I Have to Answer?

Opportunity knocks, bangs, and even whispers. Opportunity can come in one flavour or 31 flavours, but just because there are so many, does that mean you have to taste them all? Baskin Robbins has 31 flavours, but it doesn't mean you have to scramble to try them all just because they have all those flavours and they close at 6 p.m. They all look good, and I'm sure they all taste pretty fabulous too, but is that the point? Well, the point depends on the goal. Was your goal to try all 31 flavours before closing, or was it to try a new flavour in your favourite cone that day?

This same principle applies to marketing opportunities. One of my clients was asked by an event planner to organize a series of events. These events would be marketed to corporate executives—she wouldn't even have to find the market, it was already there for her. It seemed like the perfect opportunity for more business exposure, until she began excavating deeper. What she found was that as wonderful as it seemed, she had no passion for it. This "perfect opportunity" drained her every time she thought of organizing the events. Eventually, she chose to close that door. She did it with a heavy heart because she was thinking in terms of "shoulds" and not in terms of her values and that the project had nothing to do with those values—it was just a good opportunity, and one that wasn't right for her.

Aspiring actors want to have Oscars and reach star status mainly because it gives them the opportunities to pick and choose the roles and projects that are congruent with their nature, their core, their values. They don't act simply for the money and they don't choose every single script that comes their way.

Why can't we as organic entrepreneurs begin the way we want to end up, taking projects and initiatives that are in line with who we are, even if the money isn't immediately evident? We can. What happened to this client less than a month later was that she got another opportunity more closely in line with where she wanted to go and who she was. Oddly enough, it still had to do with offering events to corporate executives. This time, she was in charge and had lots of creative insights and energy to execute those ideas.

When an opportunity comes knocking, first ask who's at the door. Does the opportunity fit the moment and your values, even if it's a stretch or isn't a stretch? Did you gather all the information you could about the opportunity and the potential impact it could have on your current business environment? Do you know what level of commitment it would take to entertain the opportunity? You have to ask a ton of questions about the opportunities that come your way. Ask so many that you border on irritating because once you invite the opportunity in, it changes the pattern of your life and could even change your direction. You can always turn back from an opportunity, but you risk negatively affecting the source as well. It's better to ask more questions in the beginning and be very clear about what you want out of the commitment and what the investment could cost you in terms of your resources.

Pick your opportunities like you pick your battles: not all are worth fighting and not all opportunities are worth opening, no matter how loudly they knock.

Sun Worship

Living in Canada, I sometimes see the winter *hanging on* for weeks, even months, longer than normal. It frequently likes to keep a stubborn hold on everything, attempting to imprison everyone in its dreary spell. Ah, but relent it must to spring; and just as the seasons must relent one to the other and accept, grudgingly or graciously, the natural changes, so too must we as entrepreneurs relent to the changes we face at the end of spring—the end of "endless" creation and energy—and accept the release of greater control over to summer, where momentum must do its work.

I have long since been convinced that business is one way to be of tremendous service to humanity and a way to worship the God-given ability to be self-sufficient and to share love. Springtime in my business makes me remember this. And so when I hit a serious crisis in my business, I force myself to look deeper, past the illusion of my business as just a place to work and make money, and I see the crisis for what it really is: not the signal of the end of my enterprise, but a signal in the changing of the seasons.

Summer

Capitalism covers us like a warm summer night. Lulled into sleep by its soft romantic murmurs, we forget, we dream of might and power; and everything we want, it seems, is a shadow in this dark night. But awake! Awake! *There is more within the dream to create—consciously manipulate the spirit of coin for all or none.*

Summer's Abundance

The essence of summer is abundance. In summer, the gentle breezes of contentment and success stroke our cheeks and carry us along with care and consideration. At times, it seems our feet don't even touch the ground; the journey becomes effortless. At other times, we can't believe the turn of events. How can this be? No bumps in the road? The bumps are there, but putting emphasis on them isn't the purpose of summer. The purpose of summer is to do your best to capture the most you can from these abundant times, to capture the flavour and the quality, the weight and the shape of things you've built. These elements of summer really become the active ingredients that give you the courage to envision the things yet to manifest and yet to be dreamed.

Summer is about expansion—expansion through abundance, creativity, communication, consciousness, community, control, and giving. These are the seven principles of sustainability that we must nurture during summer, and if we do, they will sustain us throughout the autumn and the rest of the year. They are the vital signs of a healthy, organic business and life. These seven concepts will take us through the abundance that's been created by our efforts and strengthen the road we're on during these times of heady success and high energy. During the summer, you are at your strongest, you are at your peak, and you think it could last forever.

When we choose business as a life path with any elevated level of awareness, we come to understand that business is actually meant to be a Tao, that it is a philosophy, a way of life and more than just a means of earning a living. We begin to see that business is our life and life is our business and that is why we look at the following principles as a guide to a better way to incorporate and share these aspects of our selves that just keep growing as we become master of our life and our business.

Business becomes a Tao, or flow, when there is alignment, which is facilitated by the awareness and opening of oneself to all parts of one's environment on all levels, not just the material. This means that if we have an architectural firm, we're designing buildings that are aligned with the earth, the heavens, and ourselves. The same applies if we're establishing a bakery, an ice cream parlour, or a publishing house. When we are aligned in this way, we are consciously positioning ourselves to take advantage of the natural momentum or flow within all the resources at our disposal as we incorporate them within the design of our business.

Abundance

The word *abundance* is often thrown around randomly in spiritual circles and without much thought, but I'd like to be more specific. If you ask what abundance is, many would say it means having a lot, or more than enough. But the problem with that definition is that so many of us don't know or haven't taken the time to articulate exactly what that "lot" or "enough" is made up of. This is why we set out with abundance as a target without being specific and we end up with an abundance of headaches, abundant staff turnover, abundant web traffic with no sales, etc.

Whenever I speak of abundance, I tell people to go back to their list of values and imagine themselves being filled to capacity and then overflowing with each. When you can feel the entirety of having all of that, then that is what I call abundance. Living abundantly is a continuous dance between being grounded and grateful in the now and peering with focus and knowing into the future. Finding this balance makes Cirque du Soleil look like a cakewalk. Living abundantly, especially in business, might seem challenging because of the message that we've received for years that tells us we do not have enough and that the answer to what ails us, the gift of happiness, lies in the next purchase, the next sale the next high profile interview, or the next big contract—that is, something outside of ourselves.

A new and unusual perspective on living abundantly is that you can't *acquire* it, you tune in to it. Abundance is a frequency you align yourself to when you're doing work you love and sharing it with the world through your Greater Purpose—in other words, simply by being who you are, you resonate with abundance. If you're still getting some static, you're still not tuned to the exact frequency yet. You'll have to do some tweaking and fiddling with your antennae. Here are some simple questions to guide you to tune in to abundance for your business:

- Are you giving your clients what they want? Do you know what they want?

- Are you flexible enough to change currents in the direction your business should be moving in?

- Are you really listening, and if you are, what are you listening *for*?

- Do you know what your Unique Selling Proposition is?

• Have you amplified your Unique Selling Proposition? Are you marketing loud and clear the right message to the right people?

• Are you aligned to take advantage of future profits as well as the present cents?

• Are you asking for the sale?

• Are you willing to let go of a specific outcome once you've done all you can?

• Have you completely used up and recycled all of the resources at your disposal?

• Are you completely grateful for exactly where you are, warts and all?

• Have you completely forgiven yourself for any "lost" opportunities or "mistakes" you may have made in the past?

Remember that you're in business to fulfill more than just the desire for more money—you want and intend to experience love and have a venue for self-expression and any other value you've itemized for yourself while conducting your mission or work. Understand that business is an outer manifestation of an inner desire and expression is the first challenge to getting better aligned with abundance. If we approach it from the traditional aspect that the business comes first in order to give us those things we want, then we might be moving, yes, but in which wrong direction?

Creativity

When we are being creative, it is our true self recognizing itself and bursting with the enthusiasm to express it to the world. Sounds very flowery and wonderful, doesn't it?

Creativity can, however, be quite messy. It does not line up in single file and stand at attention; it is chaotic. In order to work with creativity, we need to learn to live with this chaos. During the summer as things grow and become more abundant, you are challenged to become even more creative and deal with the mess that fosters creativity.

Everyone wants to be creative, but no one wants to deal with the mess it takes to live with creativity. If you are a writer, the mess can take the form of a block and everything you have to do to work your way around, through, over, and under it. If you're a software company, the mess can take the form of learning how to deal in a non-linear way with the energy of creativity it takes to design new applications. And if you're a printing company, the mess can take the form of wasted paper and ink used to discover new ways to print that are different from your competitors. There's no doubt that creativity is untidy; it's uncontrollable and it's unpredictable.

I have a very good friend who is the father of a teenager, "Sam," who has played soccer since he was a kid and who has a great opportunity to play the game at a professional level *if* he makes the choice now to dedicate himself. He is at a creative crossroads of his craft. For the longest while, he was the prime goalie for the team and this led him into a false sense of security about his position until it began showing up in the quality of his game. The coach noticed this and brought in another goalie, telling my friend that he wanted whichever goalie felt he owned it enough to step up and play better—and he would be the lead goalie for the season.

Sam was naturally the more talented of the goalies. He believed this saved him from the bench, but it didn't. During a particular game, one too many goals were scored on him and the coach made him sit out the next game, and then the next, and then the next. At that point, it began to dawn on Sam that the coach might never put him back in for the season. His mother began to lose interest in taking him to the games. What would be the point if he's just going to warm the bench? Sam's mother was understandably angry at seeing her son so openly penalized and made an example of by the coach.

The coach was doing his job; he needed to develop great players that could compete at a state level. Sam's mother was also doing her job of wanting to protect her son, but it was his dad's reaction that really had the biggest impact on me.

Whenever Sam's father would tell me that yet again Sam warmed the bench, something in me burst in anger. I asked him again and again what he thought about it all since he's notorious for having a level head in emotional situations, sometimes to my great frustration. He said he'd spoken to his son after the third game sitting it out and Sam was listless and down and didn't want to talk about it. My friend said he only prodded Sam a little and then left him alone, telling him that when he's feeling ready to talk about it, he might have some thoughts on how he can improve and that he's willing to listen.

Days later, he told Sam this:

Sam, this creative wall you've come up against will test how much you love the game. Yes, it sucks tremendously that you're being punished by the coach, but you've got to decide if you want to keep practicing in order to prepare even just for the *chance* to play, whether you have it in you to keep practicing to support your team *in case* they need you, and if you have it in you to keep practicing simply because you love the sport. Or you can choose to give up only because you're not getting any play time.

Our love for what we do has to be strong enough to take us through the pain, struggle, and doubt of the chaos of creativity. Creativity is not always pretty and forgiving. Creativity is love in transformation and sometimes love, with our current limited vision, can be a bitch.

At the heart of creativity is love—a love that mobilizes and magnetizes individuals as well as teams. So when spirit is employed during creativity or work, we are touching love. This is a whole different aspect that hasn't really been explored in business and cannot be exploited until we're willing to have the courage to explore it within ourselves.

During every creative journey when we encounter a demon and we do battle, the result of that battle is a quantum leap in personal transformation and it is the result of that battle that we should be harvesting within companies, not shying away from simply because it's messy. Those quantum leaps in creativity we make when facing chaos are invaluable fruits to be harvested. We grow as spiritual beings every time we face a creativity demon. If we as organic entrepreneurs could figure out how to harness that internal growth, there would be more love for the ride, more understanding, more innovation, and, of course, more profit than we could handle.

In his book *The Path of Least Resistance*, Robert Fritz discusses something called "creative tension," which exists within the journey of creating. Creative tension is the act of holding a vision of the outcome in the mind's eye or the heart while working within the physical limitations of your world to manifest an outcome, and it can be painful and extremely uncomfortable. Tension between what currently exists and the dream builds. What you do with that tension will decide the outcome of your vision. Will you seek to relieve the tension by any means possible by relinquishing your hold, jumping to another project, or getting caught up in personal dramas or will you allow the tension to hold you tight and taut until it reaches its peak, thrusting you forward into completion? The choice is always yours.

Communication

"...our feelings are our compass to the quality of our thinking or the level of our consciousness..."
—Marsha Madigan, MD, "Consciousness: A Principle-Based Paradigm for Leadership," *Business Spirit Journal*

We generally communicate what we are *feeling* even though it comes through the process of thought. Albert Mehrabian, professor emeritus of psychology at USCLA, is well known for suggesting that when we communicate a message to people, only 7% of that message is verbal in the words we use. Tone accounts for a full 38% and body language for 55% (also known as the 7%, 38%, 55% rule). With this in mind, shouldn't our focus in business be to make sure we communicate well? It isn't. We confuse sophisticated technological communication *tools* with highly evolved, quality communication. Just because we can speak without impediments, it doesn't mean we know how to communicate effectively. We think that because we *can* do it that it's synonymous with doing it *well*.

We are currently living in a time when technology is advancing faster than the mastery of our personal environment. More emphasis is put on the thing we use to communicate than what is actually communicated and how it changes the lives of the receiver and the sender.

Communication is the heartbeat of a community; it allows us to understand what drives our actions and it helps us create possibilities and co-ordinate relationships. I believe that communication in business today is driven not by this need to understand but by the singular desire to facilitate transactions—or the sale. Graphically, it looks something like this:

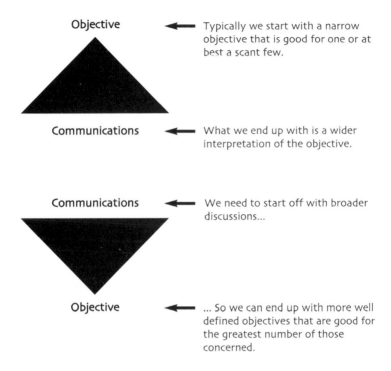

Objective — Typically we start with a narrow objective that is good for one or at best a scant few.

Communications — What we end up with is a wider interpretation of the objective.

Communications — We need to start off with broader discussions...

Objective — ... So we can end up with more well defined objectives that are good for the greatest number of those concerned.

The organic entrepreneur is more awake and realizes that communication carries with it an enormous responsibility—that responsibility is love. As we become aware of the many layers that exist within communication, we realize that it contains two essential qualities: emotion and expression. To communicate well, we must consciously develop the abilities to listen, express, question, and be patient with love.

To communicate effectively is to be heard with minimal or no "disturbance" between sender and receiver; primarily, what we're after is a clear channel between the two. Energy disturbances are missed communications, they are the resistances we feel but try to ignore and communicate over. An energy disturbance is anything that gets in the way of two people experiencing the same vision. Energy or frequency disturbances can happen due to many things: the sender's/receiver's hidden objectives, their own personal environment at the time an exchange is made, or the sender's/receiver's "baggage" at the time of reception. Your job as a conscious communicator is to minimize as many of these disturbances as you can. Here are some suggestions for balancing some of the effects of these disturbances:

If the disturbance is:	Then tune into:
Distrust	Transparency
Lack of time	Letting go of the issue for the moment
Personal emotional baggage	Humour and lightness

Every energy disturbance creates confusion and when we are confused, we shut down, shut off, or shut up, which are not what you want when you communicate. You need the natural energy from the exchange in order to grow your business organically.

The most natural place to start enabling disturbance-free communications is by cultivating your own personal environment. It shouldn't matter if you are the sender or the receiver, what matters is what's behind your perception of the message. What are your physical, emotional, mental, or spiritual challenges to communicating clearly? Are you tired, too full from a meal, too hungry, too charged, not charged enough? What are the emotional challenges that you're facing right now as you give the message? Have your buttons been pushed in another situation that you haven't yet been able to let go of? How about any mental disturbances? Are you worried about something? Do you have preconceived ideas, beliefs, or assumptions about the current environment, receiver, or message? Finally, are you connected to your own source, are you able to flow, how in touch or in tune are you to your own personal message? Since the sender is the one initiating the communication, it is their responsibility to remove as many blocks that inhibit the free flow of energy within the message as possible. This responsibility must be taken in every aspect of your business: sales, customer service, negotiations, employee relations, and your life.

You'll often hear it said that it's important to avoid emotional involvement when listening. I believe it's talk like this that not only confuses us about how to get better at communicating but it also frightens us about the power of our own emotions. Obviously, if an emotion is being triggered by something that is being communicated, it should be explored and questioned but it should never be ignored. Of course, you and the situation dictate the intensity with which you examine the feeling at that time. Ask questions such as: why am I feeling this way? Has it happened before? If so, when? Is it only with this person that I have this reaction? Is this a pattern for me when I hear this message?

The problem we've encountered so far is that we haven't been taught how to master our own domain—our own environments—in which emotions play a very important part. We've been taught to look outside for the answers and that's why we accept at face value the notion that it is beneficial to avoid involving the emotions during communications. This is only acceptable if we're still not ready to take full responsibility for the communication, and so, blame, instead of understanding, becomes a big part of communicating. We blame the other person for "triggering" us and they are therefore the "cause" of any resulting discomfort. But if we agree with this—especially in business—then we run the risk of performing an amputation of our senses, which are great tools in negotiations, public relations, marketing, and every other area of business development.

So how can we begin incorporating the emotions into business without fearing the results? The best way to begin improving communications is to assume that we know *nothing* about effective communication, especially when it comes to listening. Why? Because we are constantly changing our perspectives and our understanding. We are always changing with input from our present circumstances. If we jump into a communication with the assumption that we "know" what the other person wants, why they might be upset, or what their current needs are, then we're acting from the past, not being fully engaged in the present. Second, it cuts us off from learning because we enter into it feeling that when it comes to something as basic as listening, any fool can do it and we don't really need to relearn the basics.

Mastering listening above all takes letting go in the form of acknowledging that we know next to nothing about what is being communicated no matter how much we think we know about the person or content. When we begin to let go of our concept of our *self* while communicating, this is when we are engaged in what I call *live listening*. Live listening can only be done in the now, in the present moment that you find yourself, devoid as much as possible from assumptions and attachment to beliefs. If we are not listening live, then we are listening to validate the past or support a future directive. If we are not *live*, then we are just existing and that's not good enough to communicate the way we need to for taking products, services, and individuals to the next level.

As we rise to a new level of communication, with ourselves and with others, it is going to become increasingly important to realize that we are not just our bodies, successes, emotions, or thoughts. We are so much more and now we've got to get in touch with that "much more" in order to use business as a tool to raise the quality of life of everyone on the planet. Even if we have a successful business or we're just starting out, our quality of life and the lives of those our business touches can always be raised, improved, and refined.

It is important to know what assumptions we're operating from at all times. Our assumptions are the soil from which our communications grow and this is why starting off from our environment is so important. Communicating is like blowing dandelion seeds. With the slightest breeze, these seeds can travel great distances to lodge themselves permanently into someone else's soil—their environment.

Consciousness

I began this book with discontentment, a real hunger for something deeper, because when discontentment is married with self-awareness or consciousness it becomes a powerful driving force that initiates change on all levels of our environments.

Increasingly, within the realm of consciousness, the level of *respond-ability* (the ability to respond appropriately to any given circumstance) becomes as important as *responsibility* because it is more inclusive and empowers one to act wisely in the moment amidst unexplored experiences and territories. When we become aligned that's when we're living with synchronicity and serendipity, and we realize that the "whole" we are connected to has an infinite amount of energy that's available for us to access; we don't need to fight to get things done, get our day going, or get motivated. Whatever catalysts you use to become more connected and aware—whether it takes the form of meditation, quiet contemplation, journaling, running, Tai Chi, a few minutes of solace for reflection—are just good business practice. Use them as bookends, morning and evening, because the more deeply conscious you can become of every aspect that makes up your environment, the more you'll realize that these are the acts that hold up your life.

When I speak of consciousness in business, I am basically talking about the movement of our awareness in business in this way: *Information* ▸ *Knowledge* ▸ *Wisdom*. We are drowning in information, awash in knowledge from the "experts," and yet we are starving for true wisdom. Is it any wonder, then, that with all we have, we still feel overwhelmed and insignificant, even though we were born to be powerful and full of purpose?

As change comes upon us faster and faster, the challenge will increasingly shift from how we get more information to how we use the information we already have with greater wisdom, purpose, and love. That place where knowledge resides with wisdom is called knowing or intuition. I think it's entirely possible that as entrepreneurs and business executives, we can intuitively "know" what is right and healthy for our business in the moment. I'm not saying we need to have all the answers, but we can have access to knowledge that we're not yet aware of by being connected to our Source and to our communities.

People are becoming increasingly aware and intuitive. The only thing missing is the *language* of consciousness of which most businesses are completely ignorant—it is the conduit of effective communication. In order to speak this new language, the nature of business needs to be transformed through the conscious adjustment of the individual. Building a conscious business begins by raising the awareness level of the entrepreneur, CEO, and executive. But how does one go about raising one's consciousness and preparing for a different way of doing business, especially one that challenges enterprise as we know it? How do we let go when we're afraid of losing?

I would say that raising one's level of consciousness is really about expanding one's awareness to accept greater *possibilities* and *potentialities*. Imagine blowing a balloon larger and larger. As it expands, it touches more space and takes in more content in the form of air. What creates this expansion, if we are to equate our own consciousness with the balloon, is willingness—a willingness to be wrong (or to burst), which creates more, not less—to be challenged, to be surprised, to go beyond our current body of knowledge. Willingness leads to an awareness of our totality, of our environments of significance (cause and effect), and an awareness of never being separate or alone from anything or anyone. Ever.

"If we are to fulfill humanity's potential as stewards of a healthy, prosperous planet, each of us must connect with the seeds of our own natural desires and plant them smack dab in the middle of Wall Street and our entire economic system."
—Hal Brill, Jack Brill, and Cliff Feigenbaum, *Investing with Your Values*

Why is consciousness even a priority? Why should you, the organic entrepreneur, even be interested? Because success and thriving doesn't ever happen in the past or the future, it happens in the present. And if you're not in the present moment then where are you? You're not being fully conscious.

No matter how many forecast reports or how much historical data you compile, a business cannot be successful if it cannot act in the present. Becoming fully "present" at meetings, on sales calls, while filing documents, or just answering the phone should be the concern and mandate of every conscious business. Presence is the heart of consciousness, the seat of manifestation and personal power. We can't become better entrepreneurs if we aren't more present, even in the unpleasantness of running a business.

As business moves toward this new consciousness, we

will be increasingly convinced that the best way to moti-
vate others and increase productivity is by honouring and
discovering the spiritual underpinning of every individual
and then developing environments that support such
growth. It's important to understand that we are not trying
to shift away from the external purpose of business to this
new reality. Rather, through our growing awareness, we
are including the inner purpose of life and valuing it as
much as the profit and loss statement or market share cal-
culations. Consciousness in business demands nothing less
than compassionate capitalism.

"At last year's Business and Consciousness Conference in
Puerto Vallarta, Mexico, Michael Rennie a [McKinsey &
Company] partner from Sydney, Australia, and Gita Bellin,
a consultant with a strong metaphysical orientation, pre-
sented preliminary findings of their work with several
McKinsey clients. Their three-day process was culled from
a year's research into powerful transformational tech-
niques utilizing visualization and other elements to help
move executives from their heads to their hearts. From this
place, they then work on business issues and some amazing results have been produced in early trials.

"For instance, a telecommunications company with
a 35% turnover rate saw a 65% decrease in four months.
Several clients saw 400% productivity increases—twice the
work in half the time, as executives developed a deeper
sense of mission with an ecological and evolutionary perspective."
—Jeff Hutner, "Evolutionary Business," *Business Spirit
Journal*

If you are running a conscious business, to whom do
you answer? Who or what? Your "boss" becomes that cen-
tral place where inspiration and perspiration reside together. Your boss becomes your Greater Purpose.

One big question to guide you in your journey toward conscious entrepreneurship is to constantly ask yourself, "Is the world and my community a better place because of my business practice?" Let this be your guide in your conscious work. Another good question to help guide your progress as you become increasingly successful is, "When I consider soul and self, is one being fed more than the other?" The right answer is not one or the other but a journey toward the assembly of all parts of yourself or equilibrium. Both must be equally looked after and cared for, maybe not at the same time, but with a conscious commitment to nourishing both.

Becoming conscious in business also means neither sitting around waiting for the system to change nor ignoring the self in the development of the greater good, but instead using what Adam Smith in *Wealth of Nations* terms "enlightened self-interest," which really is the development of conscious dreams and desires while considering how they fit into a larger plan that benefits the whole as well as the parts. It doesn't just mean the parts of society in which you reside, it also means the various parts of your self: spiritual, mental, emotional, *and* physical.

The really big question therefore isn't: "How can we demonstrate that expanded consciousness in business can contribute to the bottom line?" but rather "How can we incorporate business into our ever-expanding states of consciousness to demonstrate and exemplify love in *all* its forms?" Consider that.

Momentum

Motion ▸ *Emotion* ▸ *Momentum*. It's no coincidence that these words are similar. Business is nothing if not an adventure in mastering these three things: motion, emotion, and momentum. The journey of business and the mission of being an entrepreneur are full of emotion, ups and downs and twists, action and propulsion, and often a lack of appreciation since rest can be our undoing because it seems to collide so squarely with all that momentum is about.

Navigating this inner and outer terrain is the reason why it's so important for the entrepreneur to understand that this is a conscious transformation of self. To become successful at business, we need to be willing to let the motion, emotion, and momentum of business carry us to higher ground while moulding us and polishing our character to exquisite brilliance. Maintaining momentum in business takes becoming conscious of all the factors within our environment as they work together to drive sales, relate to the public, account for profits and losses, and develop our skills as leaders.

To gain this precious momentum, we're sometimes asked to do nothing but get out of our own way. Understandably, some of the things that can hold you back from maintaining momentum can be nasty outside influences such as computer viruses that can debilitate your operation or the wrong staff that seems to spread a bad attitude like a virus. But if you dig far enough and have the courage to admit it, you'll find that the biggest block to gaining momentum is you—your thoughts and attitudes as your abilities become dulled by habit, success, and being right. And these are just some of the pests to watch out for!

So how do we continue to master ourselves while maintaining momentum?

• Make sure to check in with your Source regularly.

• Step back and gain perspective. At first glance, it may not seem that you're moving, but if you get back far enough, you'll see things are happening.

• Become more attuned to the subtleties of your environment by noticing when you shine and sparkle and how that affects both prospects and clients. Notice what time of day, month, and year this tends to happen, what you ate before experiencing certain moods, and when it's the best time for you to undertake certain projects. Remember, this is your garden.

• Find the rhythm of your business. Notice the start—stop—start—rest—rhythm of your day and work within that.

• Ground your intent. The goals you made in winter may not have set properly and could be exposed to the elements, where they could be too easily eroded. Take a moment to check in with the goals you've set in winter and see if they still resonate and, if so, how deeply.

• Is the love still alive? Check in to see that you still are loving what you do in spite of and because of the challenges and hardships. Remember if there's love, those challenges seem small in comparison.

• Are you stalled? If you are, check to see if you're giving enough. You might have become too weighed down with excess and can't move or flow freely because of the weight of all you've gained.

Momentum occurs when you're plugged in and aligned to your Source and the right resources for your environment that fuels each subsequent action. Keeping momentum going also requires juggling various skills and aspects of your life.

Have you ever seen someone precariously balance ten plates on ten tiny reeds? Never mind the million shattered pieces on the ground, those were just for practice. Keep focused on the ten plates and you'll know what it's like to be living the life of an organic entrepreneur. The greatest juggling acts of all time are performed everyday by thousands of organic entrepreneurs around the world. This is because we're juggling emotions, fears, dreams, reality, family, errands, success, failure, and our own personal development. We are contortionists, jugglers, and court jesters. We are definitely odd creatures.

For me right now, it's getting close to Christmas and here are the plates I've got in the air: a full-time college course; emotions that overwhelm and frustrate, amaze and mentally stretch me; I sent my daughter off to another continent to be with her father for Christmas; juggling emotions of abandonment, loss, and guilt; a deadline for a new keynote to a bank; the creative challenge of finding the time to design a website while feeling joy at a huge breakthrough in my career; writing a second book; creative blocks, frustration, and trying to resist the intense desire to judge my current work against the first. You see what I mean, and those are just a few. When we start throwing in the extremely volatile elements of a romantic relationship, money issues, or health conundrums, the whole scene can get quite dicey. Since life happens, what's an organic entrepreneur to do?

Throw in a monkey and you could take the whole show on the road, but, well, that would be another business altogether then, wouldn't it? Okay, so forget the monkey. Juggling is a significant part of being an organic entrepreneur. You are trying to thrive in business while staying true to your core; that's a tough act. I have found that the most important leap I made was to acknowledge this one simple truth. When it gets to be too much, however, time becomes the key—slowing time down to be exact.

The following exercise might seem counterintuitive, but it actually works: sit in a quiet place and imagine the plates are all labelled with your various challenges: relationships, your kid's new school, reviews, articles, websites, etc. See them spinning at the necessary speed to remain balanced, but instead of frantically running from one to the other spinning like a mad person, see yourself breathing deeply, evenly, and walking to each one and spinning them with ease. There, see them now all balanced perfectly—so are you. If you need to remove one of them, do so calmly, and you will find the way to tactfully remove one, or miraculously keep them all spinning successfully until you complete a project.

In case you hadn't guessed it yet, what separates organic entrepreneurs from traditional entrepreneurs is that we consciously engage our faculty of imagination a lot. By using the imagination through visualization, we can greatly reduce any trauma caused by juggling—otherwise known as life.

Connecting and Collaborating

"We are not talking about relationships in terms of networking and the like. Rather we are talking about genuine relationships based on authenticity and care."
—Roger Lewin, "The Reality of Complexity," *Business Spirit Journal*

The networks we create are of two kinds: the visible and the invisible. The visible networks are made up of those people in our database. The invisible network is created by being of real service without thought of compensation: true tithing (which is the mother of philanthropy), charity donations, and in-kind giving. Giving creates unseen connections. These acts make quantum leaps in space and time, building on the positive, building attraction, building invisible structures. It is here that we enter the domain of the soul.

The domain of the soul is almost exclusively ignored in the realm of medicine and business; soul exists in the connectedness of every aspect of ourselves, each other, and our personal environments. Its influence on our lives should not be ignored.

Why is it that as adults we have such a hard time being a part of a team environment? Why do we have such a hard time connecting? Put a bunch of adults who don't know each other in a room and tell them that they need to form groups to work on something and you'll see the eyes darting, seeking escape, hiding, and people trying to fade into the wallpaper. Why? What's so hard about being part of a team that the mere thought of coming together makes many entrepreneurs uncomfortable?

This question came to me during a course I took recently. We were told that we would be required to develop teams to finish a large project since everyone had varying levels of web design skills. One month into the program, and no one had made the slightest move to build a team even though, for the most part, we all got along. I found it odd that here we were, web developers, people who supposedly love the net for its connectivity and community, and yet no one wanted to get together on a fundamental level to build projects. Everyone wanted to be the star—alone.

Where would we be if bees thought like that? We wouldn't have honey, beeswax, honeycombs (including the cereal), nor would we have propolis, a powerful traditional medicine. Sure the queen bee is the focus of the hive, but it happens as a natural selection, not through an imposition of the will. In a team environment, the natural project leader will emerge. It became increasingly clear to me that even though these people all work on the most connected beehive in the world, the Internet, most of them were missing the point in a big way—it's about connecting, folks!

As a writer, my environment can become quite solitary. I took the course to connect and to learn more about what makes great websites work and how I can contribute my creative skills to make the Internet an even better place for my clients and visitors. As my queries to build a small team were met with blank stares and meaningless grunts, I slowly began retreating into my own writer's shell—not all the way, though. I continued to press different individuals tentatively until I finally found the trick: I began helping them for no reason. Whenever someone had a question about a problem I knew something about, I'd offer to help them figure out their challenge. Slowly, I connected with another person who helped me, and then we had a shy foreign student join our group too. Eventually, we had our team—we were collaborating.

At the heart of every great project is a team. At the heart of every great team is the individual who's willing to donate a part of themselves for the advancement of the greater project. But it's not always easy. Even though there are tools available, you need to be open and willing to use them.

Help Is *Virtually* Around the Corner

She appeared like a superhero in heels! Not that I knew what she looked like, I lived in Cambridge, Ontario, and she lived in Racine, Wisconcin. Who was this wonder woman? Her name is Roxie Hickman and before I hired her, this was my life: send out press releases, make changes to packages, send out packages, write both newsletters to my entire database, edit newsletters, send out newsletters, create special-offer e-mails, send out special-offer e-mails, write next book, speak at company event, follow up with company via phone, send thank-you note, fix broken links on website, plan a book tour, change content on website, promote website, and on and on it went. Oh, and did I mention that it's 7 p.m. and dinner isn't even a thought yet? I was literally pulling out my hair. Eventually, I followed a nudge I'd been having for months to hire someone to help me. I needed help. I decided to find myself a virtual assistant, someone who could assist me without the overhead.

I realized I didn't have enough work for someone to be physically present eight hours a day, five days a week, and I didn't have the cash flow to pay someone that kind of salary, not even part-time. The only thing that had been stopping me from hiring someone was the fee, but at $35 per hour at eight hours per month, she was worth her weight in gold because when I discovered what she did for my business and my sanity, I couldn't afford *not* to have her as part of my team.

I did some research on the Internet and found VirtualU, a very helpful site on the industry of virtual assistants and a source for finding one. You can hire a virtual assistant for any amount of time per month or per project. Their typical fee is $35 per hour and they can reside anywhere in the world. They can make calls on your behalf, mail out packages, maintain your website, and can even manage your files and desktop remotely. They can do anything an assistant can do, only they do it at a distance.

I narrowed it down to two candidates and asked questions related to what inspires them, why they do it, and what particular skills make them the perfect fit for my business. It was tough, they were both amazing, but what made Roxie stand out was how she gave more than I asked for. She sent me to a particular webpage at VirtualU where I could download and listen to real life experiences of how other entrepreneurs had received benefits from their virtual assistants and how they build relationships with them.

Roxie stood out because she had a passion for dealing with the media and she'd even worked a bit in the industry. Within two months of hiring her, she got me hired for two speaking gigs, helped me launch my book tour, and basically kept my hands out of my hair. I have found her to be an invaluable resource because having her on board means I have to use her well; I can't give her random projects without making sure that it's the thing to focus on at the moment, which ensures that it's the best possible use of her time. Having her on board makes me accountable to more than myself, and it forces me to justify those jobs I do choose to delegate to her.

Before Roxie came on board, I found myself working on countless projects. I gave them all priority (a sure sign of insanity) but made little progress, and not always in the desired direction. After I hired her, I charted my goals and objectives on a huge piece of paper and kept it on the wall in front of me, and every time I thought of giving her a job, I made sure it reflected an objective. Along with her bill, she sends me via e-mail an outline of all she's done for the month. She also calls once a week to stay in touch, follow up, and make sure she's on track with the tasks she's been given.

Sure, $35 per hour isn't cheap, but you're not hiring them for forty hours a week either. Start at three or five hours a month and you'll be amazed at the time and peace of mind you gain. You should hire someone you definitely get along with, have a connection with, and who's motivated to assist in the development of your business. Be willing to make allowances for time zones and communication errors because they do happen. Also be prepared for differences in character because as wonderful as you are, there might be days you don't see eye to eye.

How to Collaborate in Business with Anyone

If you are one of those rare individuals who has complete freedom to navigate your business without the help or need of anyone else, then you don't need to read this part any further. If, however, you are like the rest of us and need to collaborate to survive, then read on!

We all encounter various restrictions either upon us or our business at one time or another. One partner thinks it best to veer in a different direction based on market research and another wants to continue doing exactly what they've been doing based on a "gut" feeling. We also have legal restrictions to consider in any endeavour. No matter how much I would love to create a business dictated by whatever I want, I have to remember that first and foremost this business is a place of discovery for everyone, not just for me.

At some point I'm sure you are going to be engaged in a business disagreement with someone, and regardless of your personal feelings about them, you're going to be compelled to win. Here are some tips and perspectives to help ensure you *both* win and get what you want:

Test your environment

You know what you want. At some point before the issue becomes one driven by emotions, casually mention your ideas as though they were just thoughts—something like "You know I was just thinking, wouldn't it be cool to do…" or "What are your thoughts on…?" The more "matter of factly" you introduce it, the more direct and natural a response you'll receive. The goal isn't to get an immediate green light to your ideas at this point—but to take it if you do!—the whole point of this fishing expedition is to gauge the other party's level of support or resistance to your idea.

Get their input and ideas

Whether casually or more pointedly, ask them for their ideas. What would they do in such a situation? How would they do it and why? Doing this also gives you the time (but you don't know it yet) to assimilate any logical or reasonable perspective you may have overlooked, and if this turns out to be the best recourse, then accepting it will be that much more harmless to your ego—let's be honest, this probably is the biggest thing at stake! And even if you're not big enough to admit it, others do have good ideas too.

Ask for their help

There are enough problems being an entrepreneur, so don't try and create them all yourself. You'd be amazed how amenable others can become to your approach if they're made to feel useful. Ask for the help of someone who's gone through similar trials themselves—and listen.

Do the due

...the due diligence that is. When you're advancing with intention, be sure to come into the game with some understanding, some good research about your market, a few financial forecasts, and a case history or two. Do not leave anything to the imagination. You'd be amazed at how different one project can be envisioned by two separate people and how ineffective words can often become in describing a dream.

Level the emotional with good common sense

Always back up your ideas by stating how they will benefit from a logical, rational purpose. Good, solid common sense objectives are: productivity, efficiency, operating below your means, acting in line with your mission, vision, and values, and lifetime value of client relationships.

Gather support

Do you have access to friends, experts, executives, or influential figures whose views might support your plan? Is it possible to get them to speak on your behalf? Look for case studies or articles that support your perspective.

Cost backup

Make sure you have other alternatives to go on in case the cash flow or a loan aren't what you expected. Always leave yourself with options.

Don't rush for resolution

Whenever you have two opposing energies, there always exists a natural tension and the common tendency is to seek a resolution to the discomfort, the unknown, the fear—A.S.A.P.! Resist the urge to do this. Give everyone involved time to assimilate your plan or ideas. Given time, a lot could change, including opinions—even yours. Leave everything out in the open, sitting in plain sight for a week or two with no attachment to the outcome.

Choose the moment

Select a mellow moment when it isn't a problem if a disagreement were to erupt and spill out over a couple of days. Avoid a confrontation on the way to an event or meeting where you're going to have to force yourself to suppress your opinions and feelings. Also avoid similar discussions if you are tired, hungry, or already upset about something else.

Keep it in context

Don't bring up old issues, and keep the discussion to the issue at hand.

Start out light and flexible

Resist the urge to say things like: "Are you out of your mind?! That idea sucks!" The biggest killers of any plan are wild personal accusations.

Present the plan

Throw into your discussion the reasons why you believe your project or plan is worth doing.

Show some emotion

Don't be afraid to get emotional while pleading. Show your human side when you exclaim, "I've always dreamed of building something like this since I was a child!" or "I think a project like this really speaks to the talent of what we can create as a team!"

Try to avoid bringing others into the mix

Unless the issue specifically involves an outside party, leave the outside where it belongs: out there.

Best-case scenario

You're a hit and it's been given the green light! They love you and your ideas and you have unlimited approval for all aspects of the plan.

Real-life scenario

They have a ton of changes, things they hate about it, and a bunch of reasons (foolish or otherwise) that they think it won't or don't want it to work. The bottom line: you got approval to engage something close to your original plan. Everyone is content with the results and you still have a healthy relationship with all involved.

Worst-case scenario

They are right and you aren't. What next? Some possible options: rant, sulk, kick a hole in the door, retreat to the restroom for a good meltdown, agree to the changes, *or* resume discussions with a willingness to relent on some changes, change your perspective, or try to come back with a better idea. If a project is worthwhile, you will find a way to get it done.

Winning – The Highs and Lows

In the summer, you'll find you're winning a lot. I can remember when I gave my first succession of public presentations—it was amazing. I received lots of positive feedback about the topic, names of potential clients, and other possible speaking engagements also came out of it. I was flying high, but the withdrawal hit two days later.

Although I had spent weeks preparing for a new talk, when it finally came time to do it, I felt lost because I hadn't memorized it. I decided to abandon that talk and come up with another one—and fast. This left me wide open and vulnerable but fully in the moment and able to speak from my heart to theirs. I was open to giving and receiving and what I got back was an energy *surge*. Great, right? On its own, yes, it was, but taken in the context of the whole business, I didn't manage it well.

When Monday came, I just couldn't get it together. I was still high as a kite but felt listless and dragged my butt doing all the things that were scheduled for that week, mainly writing and taking care of myself. I did a poor job of dealing with the day-to-day activities because I was still craving the high.

I'm not alone. Not that this is any more comforting, but it happens to many individuals after a trade show, summit, or seminar. Statistics show that most companies don't follow up on the leads they receive at trade shows. What's up with that? Don't we all want more business, especially when having a booth at one of these events is so expensive to begin with?

I've discovered that winning brings with it a unique set of circumstances and challenges. As with plants, life above the soil is a whole different experience. For a plant, the sun brings nourishment, but too much exposure to it without having the internal mechanisms to manage that light could be harmful. For an entrepreneur it's the same, winning is a wonderful aid, but knowing how to manage it is even more important.

Managing our wins can be as simple as taking a morning off, increasing our vitamin intake, getting out for more fresh air, or sharing more. It doesn't need to have anything to do with your to-do list, your agenda, or your Palm Pilot. For me, helping my daughter with her art project was what I needed at that moment to manage the win and come back to a place of balance; I was still exchanging energy by helping her, but it wasn't as turbulent.

Coming off a winning high with grace is about balance and equilibrium within ourselves because winning can bring out the best and the worst in all of us; these are the circumstances and challenges I mentioned. When we win, we almost always lose or shed something else. It could be an old belief, shyness, immaturity, or we could lose something as essential as our way. Like Hansel and Gretel, make sure you leave some crumbs on the path of your journey in business so that you can always turn back, to remember why you started this and who you truly are.

Control

To build more caring, profitable, efficient businesses, we have got to embrace the chaos and general disturbances that aligning with our Greater Purpose in business brings and this means letting go of our need for control in every area.

The lessons of business are mainly about attitude, teaching us not only about our greatness but also our need for humility, grace, and respect for all things. At a certain point, business teaches us to give up our illusion of control. Can we give up those aspects of our business that we believe we've molded with our bare hands, created out of nothing? Would that open us up to chaos? I believe it opens us up to wonder and miracles. Isn't that what happens when we plant a business idea and then that idea begins to interact with other random thoughts?

We steadfastly believe that balance is about control, but control of what? Nine times out of ten, the answer is control of our own personal environment and not some external force. But how many times do we acknowledge this as the factor when faced with an accident, financial pressures, family issues, or relationship challenges? How many times do we say in these situations that we're going to choose to *direct* our emotions or our thoughts in a certain way? How many times do we decide beforehand we're going to regulate and bring ourselves back on course by expelling something, whether it's anger, depression, frustration, apathy, or a person. How many times do we decide to consciously reduce the spread of a specific element in our life and our business instead of waiting until another healthier alternative is forced on us and then struggling with the controls? Not often enough. But as organic entrepreneurs, we must learn how to auto-regulate our own environment if we are to be successful from the inside out. "But stuff just keeps happening. I can't do anything about that," you say.

Internal incongruities between our environment and our control gauges typically cause the problems we have with outer realities. These gauges help regulate the flow of energy or stimulus and include proper breathing, slowing down, living in the present, laughter, sleep, intimacy, and touch, to name just a few. Somehow these controls get misaligned, out of tune, and we stop acting in accordance with our divine nature or with our values. This is when the wires get crossed and we end up being pushed in all different directions, becoming the victim of circumstances and situations we believe are out of our control. But the truth is, most of these situations *are* within our control, but we need to listen and act sooner.

But how do you master the effective use of controls in your environment? By acknowledging your current reality, by expelling non-productive energies, by storing beneficial energies by making adjustments (even miniscule), by accepting, by listening, by keeping a close eye on your feelings, your intuition, your thoughts, the choices you make, and by acting on what you know is true for you and therefore also right for your business.

The control switches are there to help us fine-tune our brand, our mission, our vision, our service—and ourselves, but we need to be in the cockpit, not out in the cabin serving cocktails.

Grounded in Gratitude

There is not a way to gratitude, gratitude is the way.
–Mahatma Ghandi

Imagine for a moment that you have just accomplished the biggest dream of your business: you closed the biggest deal; you landed your company a spot on the hottest national television show, or, as it was for me not too long ago, you landed a publishing contract. Go ahead, imagine it in all its glory. Now imagine you achieve this very dream (or something even better) today or tomorrow. Do you think your body would go through the same routine it goes through on any normal day? Not a chance! You're pumped with energy, you run around doing "stuff" but get little done, your palms sweat, your heart races, you can't sleep, you can't focus, you worry you're not doing the right things perfectly—in a nutshell, you're wasting precious time. This could go on for days, weeks, or (shudder) even months until you finally get your bearings back.

In moments like these, our bodies go through a power surge. It's heady, intoxicating, and as potentially destructive as being hit by lightning, but it can all be minimized (notice, I didn't say avoided) by grounding ourselves in our soil through gratitude.

Nowadays, all electrical outlets have what's called a ground wire. This wire goes deep into the ground and acts as a stabilizer to disperse any sudden surges in power. This makes good sense, right? Then why don't we ground ourselves as our businesses continue to expand? Probably because we don't know that we can do anything at all to unplug ourselves while we're occupied by the energy surge.

After I got over the initial impact of "Oh my gosh, somebody actually wants to publish my words!" I thought I had it together. Not so! I continued to "drift," as I call it, not really being connected to my core and doing a million things that didn't really have to be done. For months after the news, I just went through the motions of daily tasks, but I knew I wasn't fully living the dream because I had experienced a power surge and didn't know how to stabilize myself. When I finally did, it was with the grace of three things: family, faith, and fun.

Let me explain: my family was always my outward source of strength and so I spent more time with them even if my mind told me I really needed to be doing this or that on the computer. I strengthened my spiritual core by reconnecting and improving on my daily spiritual exercises instead of cutting back as things became more pressing. I made myself have more fun. I began seriously dating again and goofing around more and just being more lighthearted instead of bogging down my spirit with all the important "work" that *had* to be done. It came down to the basics.

When we sit on the floor, our body naturally avoids falling over as it finds some point of reference, or centre. At some point during our frenzy, we need to take mini-breaks and get in touch with a similar centre and ground our progress in something more than just the next big coup. We need to remind ourselves that it is from this centre, from which we've grown, that we are still growing—we need to come here, back to the present, to continue building through success.

Grounding—coming back to the present and being grateful—can easily be done by naming things around you. For example, name everything you see: your favourite pen, your writing book, a purple piece of scrap paper, the cordless phone, a red folder, the laptop. Then look around and do the same thing: a glass of juice, two candlesticks, the tree outside, the birdfeeder, the bricks of your house, all the while breathing slowly and deeply. What this simple exercise does is bring you back to your present reality; it forces the swirling to stop or at the very least slow down as you consciously focus on what's right in front of you.

After a while, you'll notice the rise and fall of your breathing and from here you can actually slow it down some more in addition to finding gratitude, an essential quality of being grounded. You may find gratitude for your success, your strength, and your freedom—you'll slow down long enough to realize that you're actually having fun...or not. Either way, you'll find truth.

When considering grounding through gratitude, we think that it's the easiest thing to do: to be grateful. But try doing it when you're on a high and you think the world is your oyster. Try being grateful for just being able to breathe when you have more money in your bank account than you've ever made in your whole working life combined. Trying being grateful for all the colours you can actually see with the naked eye when you can afford a pair of sunglasses worth $1,000. Try being grateful that you have the resources and have cultivated an environment that attracts great staff when you can hire any top gun from any firm you choose.

Gratitude is easy when you're struggling, but it can be a whole other ball game when you've "made it." The thing about "making it" is that it comes with the assumption that there's nothing else, that you've gone as far as your imagination can take you, and that you are unbreakable.

Gratitude grounds us in the smallest things we take for granted every day. Gratitude is saying thank you to your customers, your mentors, your nemesis, your family (for putting up with your strange hours), the food that sustains your energy, the time, the money, and something greater than you for those things given to you without your knowing. Just say thank you—and mean it.

Everyone wants to know that they've had a hand in something good, that they've been important in some way to the lives of others. When you go out of your way to say thank you, to acknowledge your gratitude for those around you, the ground you're growing in gets richer. It's as if it's been charged by the surge, thereby enriching it. People start to buzz; you might not see it or hear it, but it's happening and this, of course, creates a ripple effect with its own rewards. This ripple effect is exactly the movement that is created during the summer: it's an outpouring from you to your environment as you nourish those around you. Gratitude is a form of sharing and it makes us lighter, but its effect benefits everyone it touches.

In times like these, just remember to be grateful about what's right in front of you, what's right, and what's true. Nothing is worth losing your grounding for. All the excitement and self-importance may shake you for a moment, but don't let it erode the precious soil where you're planted.

Giving

The current trend is to keep as much as you can for as long as you can, but I'll say this: you can't soar if you're chained to the ground. Hoarding, whether it be praises, thanks, wealth, people, innovation, ideas, power, or any resource you've come to be very good at mining, is the equivalent of being in shackles.

Now, this doesn't mean you shouldn't plan for the

future or invest—these are, of course, vital to the survival of your business. As an organic entrepreneur, it's essential to become more conscious of the built-in mechanism that alerts you to when you're spiritually, mentally, emotionally, and physically "full." You can determine this by asking yourself: "When is enough enough for my standards, my values, and my vision? When do I start giving back, and how do I give back?" Any bounty that is given to us in life is to be shared—freely given out in order for us to go even further or we risk stalling, blocking, and stagnating. Giving helps you stay afloat. I think this concept needs to be addressed at the very onset of one's business and not tacked on at the end when you've become so successful you start to feel guilt nipping at your heels. Guilt should never be the motivation for giving; you should plan to give from a place of love and not from fear or guilt.

Planning to give makes it easier to do when you're full of deadlines and stretched as is typical during the summer and it ensures you don't use your circumstances to decide whether you should give or not. If you can plan to receive from your customers then you can plan to give back as well. If you can plan your next year's sales forecast, then you can plan to give 10% of it away to a cause that everyone in the company can believe in and support. If you can plan to hire three new salespeople, then you can plan for the company to be a part of initiatives such as Habitat for Humanity or Meals on Wheels. Like good communications, positive collaboration, and gratitude, giving doesn't just happen on its own, it needs to be consciously initiated.

When you're thriving, at a time of such high energy, it might be tempting to think that what's needed is more action, but it's actually the opposite. What's needed in the phase of summer is simplification and this is another reason why we give during this time. Think about it: the lighter you are, the greater momentum you can expect from your efforts.

Now, if you've never really planned for giving within the first year of your business, you can still do so. Here are some ways you can structure your business for giving naturally:

• If you're a sole proprietor, decide from the beginning which organization you'd like to donate either your time or a portion of your funds to. If you instead have staff, once a year get everyone together and ask them what their own favourite charities are and as a group decide which one gets your attention or funds this year.

• Align your business from the beginning with a cause and work collaboratively with that cause throughout the life of your business. It could be that $1 of every sale goes to your chosen organization. This way, when you grow, they grow and it lends a sense of foundation to your business, a solidity that is hard to buy as your business matures.

• Dedicate a specific amount of your time or that of someone on your staff to register the impact of your contribution and communicate that to your staff and your community.

• Reinvest in well-researched, socially responsible investment avenues when it comes to that time when your business is making enough money that you can afford to save some of it.

• Set aside a portion of corporate funds for the mental, emotional, and spiritual health of those who work for you. By this I mean develop a fund that your staff can use if they need mental therapy, family counselling, sabbaticals, or some other spiritual release that rejuvenates them after having worked for you for many years.

• Keep a log of all the positive things that either you or your staff have accomplished throughout the year. Never let a year go by without praising yourself and those around you for their time, attention, and for contributing part of their spirit toward the advancement of *your* dreams.

One last thing about giving that I think many people and businesses don't get is that it should be done without the expectation of receipt at any point in the future and without any expectation of how it should be received. If we can't let go when we give, then it's not giving, it's a loan and the benefits are not quite the same. There's a time and a place for a loan and there's a time and a place for giving.

Just as the summer season gives us her fruits, if we are wise, we will also give back our own abundant gatherings whether in service or coin. This keeps the balance and helps prepare us much better for the coming capriciousness of autumn.

Autumn

What we reap in autumn is what we believe in our bones without a shadow of doubt.

Autumn's Economy

Change. It is the essence of autumn. It is a time when all you thought you knew about your business and yourself seems to do an about-face, taking you in unplanned directions or challenging you to alter a long-held belief or perspective in order to prepare you for the long term.

The winds of autumn shake to the ground the superfluous, the overripe, and the immature. So too will the autumnal winds of business shake free everything that isn't needed for the next phase; it will cast off those projects, goals, and assumptions that have seen their time and those that do not have the strength to survive the long, harsh winter to come.

As you grow your business, you understand your past and build an appreciation for why you went through the experiences necessary to enrich your soil with the wisdom that understands what is good for the world. You begin to trust that you do indeed have the elements necessary to build a thriving business and that the world does indeed need what only you can offer. You begin to trust that someday, when the season is right and the winds are favourable, your business will emerge to create a profitable synergy between a ready market and a useful product or service that changes individuals for the better, that transforms and lifts them beyond their current state of consciousness.

During the autumn, there is an emphasis on maturity and completion. It's a time for reflection, cooling or slowing down, and conservation. There is a waning of our strength, which we try to hold onto or are quick to regret, but it happens for a reason: preservation. Like every other season, autumn has its own unique events and insights. If we listen carefully, it is trying to teach us more about *self* management, how to structure personal environments for maximum energy and efficiency, the *responsibility* of economics and freedom.

Each person's path toward a conscious business will be different from the next person's, mainly because of the makeup of our inner being and how we perceive and interact with our world with its losses, challenges, bounty, and energy. In essence, discovering the path toward conscious entrepreneurship is about discovering yourself and mastering the elements of your own personal environment.

Personal Environments

Our personal environment is our world. Take a look:

Our Environment

Health
Thoughts
Feelings
Actions
Dreams
Diet
Rest
Exercise

Personal Expression
Painting
Lighting around you
Journaling
Gardening
Telling more truth
All senses
Failure

Money
Saving
Blocks around
Money
Giving
Gratitude
Spending
Investing
Will

Source

Relationships
Partner/Spouse
Friends
Children
Earth
Self
Your Source
What you believe

Education/Knowledge
What you watch
Read
Experience
Letting go
Dreams
Dialogue
Innocent exploration
Asking more questions

At the centre of it lies you and your Source; everything else that surrounds it—your kids, your work, your hobbies, your spouse, your furniture, friends and pets—is your environment. There are five major elements that make up anyone's environment. They are: health, personal expression, education/knowledge, relationships, and money. I have come to realize, through many years of coaching, that there is a direct relationship between the vibration rate of our personal environment and the quality of business we are engaged in. And the more we cultivate our core, the more synergy there is between our business and our personal environment. The *value* of the core dictates how you *resonate* with all five of your environment through *cohesion*. The equation looks like this:

Value + Resonance + Cohesion = the Quality of
Your Personal Environment

Let me explain what I mean:

Value is the significance you assign to an element within your environment, like beauty, innovation, or order.

Resonance comes from the Latin and means to "return to the sound." Imagine that everything we do and think, good or bad, moral or immoral, is a wish to discover and unite with that sound. Our unconscious goal is to return to the source of this sound. Although we may identify with the object or the form the sound takes: a man or woman, a pet, a possession etc., the truth of the attraction is the resonance we remember when in the presence of that being or thing. The experience vibrates within and around us like a tuning fork and becomes a sonic homing device confirming our inner direction. Resonance develops between objects that have the same frequencies of vibration or rhythm that are within close proximity. When the two near each other they will draw closer and unite at the level set by the stronger of the two vibrations. Therefore your highest vibration drives the elements that are drawn to or repelled from your environment. What drives or dictates the frequencies within your environment? Is it love, money, fear, anxiety or self-expression?

Cohesion is the "glue" that transmits the communication and the stronger the glue the more powerful your reach and attraction.

By using the example of a tuning fork and a piano, the principle of resonance can be explained this way: strike a tuning fork keyed to the note of B, then upon lifting the lid of the piano, softly searching among the piano wires, you would find the B note piano wire vibrating. This is because the vibrations of the tuning fork triggered a like response in whatever is closest that has a similar frequency.

The way something vibrates establishes its form. Therefore, if you want to have better experiences with your clients and your business (or anything, for that matter), then look at ways to change, specifically to increase, your own personal vibration. When you are communicating you are creating resonance between yourself and another. When you are communicating harmoniously and both of you are getting what you want out of the experience, then you are creating sympathetic resonance. Being "in tune" or "on the same wavelength" are both terms that illustrate sympathetic resonant relationships or experiences. The fastest way to improve resonance within your environment to change or grow your business is through conscious love and service. Love what you do so much that you vibrate with it and have an overwhelming desire to serve others as much as yourself and your family. I'm not saying this is the only way to change or grow, but it's one of the fastest ways.

So if we're not creating resonance, then what are we creating? If it's not resonance, it's "environmental noise" or dissonance. Dissonance happens when energy oscillates between two or more forms without coming together to form one sound. The waves just continue to beat against one another. When dissonance becomes resonance, there is a state of resolution. Our conscious awareness of dissonance, resolution, and resonance in our daily activities serve as sonic signals or life punctuations.

Learning to listen to, differentiate, appreciate, and interpret these signals in your life is fundamental to a healthy personal environment and is what makes you and your company become extremely adaptable to change, not to mention highly conscious and profitable.

At some point during your personal transformation and after your intentional commitment to a conscious business, you're going to begin feeling a healthy compulsion to attract different clients, suppliers, and advocates to your environment. In this bio-electrical field that is your personal environment, you manifest a healthier, stronger, more adaptive business because it has suddenly become a more environmentally intelligent organism—a complex adaptive system.

Becoming an organic entrepreneur means undergoing a conscious transformation. I have a coaching client that owns a thriving massage therapy, yoga, and healing arts practice. Before we began working together, she would frequently be overcome with guilt about taking some much needed time off because she had to turn clients away and she was afraid that clients would migrate to another practitioner and that she would eventually lose business.

After some time working on adjusting and clearing up her own personal environment, she came to realize that what she needed to do was *educate* her clients so they would understand that she needed to take time away regularly. This was in order to give optimal service, since the healing profession takes a lot out of the practitioner, and she couldn't perform optimally if she felt burnt out.

We wound up with a plan to design a message for her answering machine a week to ten days before her departure, notifying clients of her upcoming absence. Another way of helping her adapt to her thriving business was to put this information straight on her website so future clients would know and already be prepared that this is how she practices. This prevented a lot of stress and anxiety over having to turn anyone away because if they did not return, that would simply mean they were not the best clients for her at the time and not the best elements for her environment.

To have a successful, healthy business on all levels—one that resonates with our highest purpose—we need to cultivate a profound understanding of the movement of energy and the different ways that it courses through our system and the system of our business—and economics plays a vital role.

Conscious Economics

The word *economics* means "household management" and comes from the combination of two Greek words: *oikos*, meaning "house" and *nomos*, meaning "to manage." This understanding brings business back to earth, home, and hearth. Your household is your entire domain.

I can't write about what it takes to be a successful organic entrepreneur and not write about money. Nearly all of us have emotional responses to money—good or bad. And since 99% of our emotional responses to money have nothing to do with money and everything to do with the relationship we have with ourselves, it is in the best interest of our business that we deal with any buried issues about money. If you have any attachments to money at all, you have an issue with it. But I want to highlight for you that there's nothing *wrong* with having an issue with money; what's "wrong" or unhealthy is not knowing about it and therefore not being able to deal with it before it becomes a problem for your business.

I recently made a new friend thorough another good friend. She began sharing with me tales of how she courageously battled the effects of cancer and she said, "I don't know if you've ever had to deal with this in your family." I said, "No I've never had to, our family has always been quite healthy." I told her, however, that in my opinion all families have their "cancers" they have to deal with. Ours was a consciousness of lacking that consistently represented itself in the form of issues with money. Don't let the personal issues that you may have with money eat away at your profits and potential like a cancer. Deal with them if you want your business to grow.

When you hear the term "having your financial house in order," it conjures an image of only the numbers—of getting one's papers together, knowing where they are, and staying on top of the accounting. But having your financial *house* in order means much more than that. At the foundation of this house once again is you, your environment, and how you relate to your core and the world. For organic entrepreneurs, a sound business economy means having their needs, wants, desires, dreams, and visions in sight 100% of the time in relation to their changing personal environment, and being able to adapt these needs to the challenges at hand. The less friction, dissonance, or "noise" there is between these things and your environment, the more clearly you can see and act on what must be done to grow, change, and adapt in order to survive and thrive.

One tool that signals a possible need to change can be found in your accounting practices, whether you do the books on your own or you sit with your accountant and do them. Accounting lets you see where there may be holes, opportunities for growth, reserves you hadn't noticed, or even how much you've grown closer to your vision. Accounting as a tool, however, is useless if the lens or framework (you) with which you interpret the signals is distorted, unclear, or out of focus.

How a company relates to its economic state is a direct result of the state of consciousness of those directing its course, which relates back to how the individuals relate to money. Do you resist hearing unpleasant news about the economic direction of your life or business? Until you clear up that resistance, you're going to be wasting precious time between when you hear the signal and when you take action—your lens could even alter what you see and hear.

An account is simply a record or narrative of events. The numbers are not trying to hurt you or flatter you, they are simply telling you a story. Your ability to respond to this story and how honest and accurate you are about your reactions to the signals the story is trying to give you will determine your level of accountability. In other words, accountability is your ability to relay the financial events of your business or life truthfully. The ability to accurately record the movement of money (accounting) is set by how well aligned your own personal values, beliefs, and Greater Purpose are with the current state of your personal environment. I often tell my clients that money is a language, and language is used to tell a story. Really, it's that simple.

Beliefs – Our Dirty Little Secret

Many of our beliefs are built around these ideas: "No one will be interested in what you have to offer or say"; "You have no experience doing any of this"; "You have no credentials"; "This isn't even making any money yet"; "You're just going to fail/get shafted/be disappointed— again"; "You can't write/act/paint/manage/lead"; "No one cares"; "You're just this little nobody, in this little room you call an office."

Awful stuff, isn't it? And the annoying thing is you can't even serve up any barbed retorts because the person speaking is you! And the *really* sad thing is most enterprises fail because of this internal, negative dialogue and not some external force such as eroding market share, poor branding or plummeting sales. What we tell ourselves on a minute-to-minute basis is our dirty little secret because most of us don't talk very nicely to ourselves when we're venturing forth into some new territory. This is as true for entrepreneurs as it is for sales and marketing teams in large corporations. The nasty dialogue you read above are things I've told myself for years—it's a miracle I succeeded at all!

Now is the time to take a look at what thoughts could be holding you back from an expanded awareness of your Greater Purpose, and therefore greater success, and then let them go. Now is the time to shed them like old skin and ask what purpose they serve. If you understand the truism that nothing comes without losing something first, then you can't escape letting go during the autumn of your business. In order to move on to greater sales, you have to let go of guilt about possibly having a lot more than those around you. You have to let go of the belief that you might lose yourself or your family if you move forward and claim greater success. You have to let go of the fear that you could fail miserably with no chance for a second take. You have to let go in order to move on.

Your internal dialogue is based on the past. That little critic knows nothing of your present or future. Admittedly, our past foreshadows a *probable* future if we continue doing the same things in the same way, but if you're an organic entrepreneur, you're not going to use the same ingredients every time you plant your seeds. You are constantly changing your patterns and altering your soil to create the best environment for growth.

If you're working so hard at changing your patterns, how do you alter the negative dialogue or get it to stop and leave you alone? Oddly enough, at first, the goal is quite the opposite. Let it talk while you listen very carefully. When it does come up, pay attention to how things are being said and be aware of the times when you want to agree. Then, acknowledge everything that's been said because at some point, it was true. Don't fight back. The best way to put it in its place is through conscious action.

Start small by writing down your negative dialogue on a large piece of paper on one side, and on the back, write down the comeback. For example, if one of your favourite personal beliefs is, "You have no experience doing this," then a possible comeback could be, "Experience starts by being willing, and I am willing."

Once you've mastered the comeback, move on to small acts of kindness that support your goals and initiatives. This way, you're not simply trying to beat it with ineffective polar opposites: "No you can't." "Yes I can." That's a waste of time. Beat it with consistent positive action that supports your dreams, goals, and intentions.

Secret destructive beliefs are compelling: they draw us in with a hint of truth, and before we know it, we're an accomplice in the death of our own dreams. But secret beliefs can only survive if we agree with them and keep them locked up. The real secret is that you are much greater than anything you've ever accomplished or failed at. This is the real glorious secret we try to keep from ourselves every day.

So what if you fail? You cannot have success in business without failure—you know that and I know that…in theory. But how many of us are willing to avail ourselves of the regenerative qualities of failure? The answer: Not too many. Failure in business is the engine that drives success and yet most of us want to divorce ourselves from it so quickly when it does happen. Instead it should be embraced, quickly reincorporated back into your business processes, and assimilated not annihilated. If we keep trying to hide our failures, pretty soon we end up with a breakdown somewhere else and more often than not, it is our health that suffers.

Your Health

An entrepreneur hears it all the time—we hear it from those around us who are supportive and even in our own heads: press on; don't give up; keep at it.

It gets to the point where sometimes we start adopting this attitude with every aspect of our lives, not just our business. Push, push, push. If it's not budging, then push harder. Pretty soon we're being this way with our bodies. You may be experiencing more frequent headaches, but you tell yourself you have a deadline and can't stop, so just take a couple more aspirins. Your back might be killing you, but since you've taken on a bigger project and hired another staff member, "it'll pass," you tell yourself, and you push it one more day, and another, and another, until you suffer a major health setback and now you're in bed for a week. What does health have to do with being a conscious entrepreneur? Everything. Especially in autumn when things tend to shift and turn on a dime and you're off scrambling in another direction. The vagaries of autumn test your fortitude and your flexibility on every level.

If you're an entrepreneur, you know that you are the waiter, chef, and dishwasher; if anything were to happen to you, the whole thing could go to hell in a handbasket pretty quickly. Some would say that's what insurance is for. I say, why wait? Why leave it up to the insurance company to take care of your most prized asset? Why not adopt a preventative perspective by taking care of yourself in small ways now?

If you still don't get it and you need an illustration, here's what I'm talking about: about two years ago, I was working for a financial services firm located about one and a half hours away from home. Each day, I would wake up at 4:45 a.m., drive three hours in total, and come home, do my writing, and coach clients, as well as take care of a teenager (need I describe the challenges of that one?).

Where was *I* in this whole equation? I don't even know where *that person* was. I did, however, find her one beautiful summer day, sprawled quite unattractively on the asphalt with blood streaming from a gaping hole that was typically filled with a front tooth. Her hand was broken in a few places and her hip was out of alignment by a few inches. What in heaven's name happened to her, you ask? Was she hit by a pickup truck? Actually, yes, that's precisely what happened. I was out walking for lunch one day, when an overzealous pickup truck mowed me down.

My health would become my number one priority in the months ahead because I had so blatantly ignored it for years. My body couldn't be silenced any longer, so it created an "accident," a scenario in which I would feel it was okay to slow down because I wouldn't have heeded any other signals such as the flu or migraines. So I, on an unconscious level, came into agreement with a situation that could help me slow down: an "accident." But the accident became a gift; it was a turning point in my career and helped me decide to begin working with more intention and commitment to my writing and coaching because that was what I loved and what gave me purpose.

Since I didn't listen to my body and I didn't take care of myself in the times when I could have, I now have aches, pains, and fears that no typical thirty-nine-year-old woman should suffer from. I can't stand for more than an hour, my neck muscles seize up if they haven't been moved regularly, my right hand that was broken feels like it has arthritis, and going for a nice walk in the outdoors is not so simple for me anymore—and traffic now scares me. Thankfully, I'm the type that feels fear and does things anyway, and now I take care of myself. Now I listen.

My point is this: the body has an inherent, divine intelligence that knows when enough is enough, even if we do not. It will create a shutdown period for you if you don't listen. Our minds and bodies working together have the power to create illnesses, "accidents," and diseases from seemingly out of nowhere. Most of the time, if we have pushed the body to this shutdown point, it takes longer to get better than if we'd just taken good care of our selves and our bodies over time. This includes taking your vitamins regularly, going for walks, enjoying time with your family (but don't just go through the motions, really enjoy their presence), and eating well, not just what's available for nuking.

Take good care of yourself because if you've hit the wall (or the pickup truck) and you're flat on your back, afraid you might never walk again, that's all that's going to matter—not the project that didn't get finished or the irate new client who could have been your cash cow for years. None of that will matter.

Treat your health—mental, emotional, spiritual, and physical—as the prime resource that it is and it will be your faithful employee.

Compassion

If we are growing organically, in line with our values and vocation, we must have compassion primarily for ourselves. For what we go through in developing a business from the germ of an idea to an enterprise that can feed more than one family, it deserves nothing less than understanding and compassion. But we so often deride and scoff at the growing pains we go through in business. We expect only the good times, the pina coladas at poolside, and the million-dollar bank account because that's where some president of a Fortune 500 company is right now in his game. But sometimes it's not rosy, it's painful.

Compassion is an odd sort of word to weave into the fabric of our business, but it is desperately needed nonetheless. Why do we have so much resistance to it, especially in business today? I think it comes back to that "V" word again: *vulnerability*. But our pains are our pains.

One of my clients is part of a fairly large family business and he's had to come to the onerous decision of letting his other siblings go from the business because they were causing more harm than good. This was excruciatingly painful for him, but this business decision is polishing his character and business acumen to a brilliance that is unmistakable. One of this client's values is success and now he can move freely in this direction, but it hasn't been without personal pain and sacrifice. During this phase of letting his brother and sisters go, he's needed a generous amount of compassion for himself. He knew what needed to be done—he had been toying with the idea for nearly fifteen years. He didn't need a cheerleader, but benevolence and compassion.

We need to remember that our pain is our gift—it is our grace—and that when we are suffering, it is our divine chance to act with grace and kindness—to customers, readers, shareholders, investors, and partners. First and foremost, however, the commitment to compassion must be to oneself. Being kind to ourselves makes the path of business much easier to bear. It makes the bank notices easier to look at, the late-paying client easier to communicate with, and your child, who's begging you to come and read a bedtime story instead of spending another night in front of your computer, more lovable. I advocate the use of compassion as an integral part of business—we should continue to *feel* even in the face of great profits, expanding markets, or plummeting stock prices.

As you watch it all unfold, it might seem like you're part of the cast in a reality show, and business can be very scary, but don't stop all feeling just because you're in business.

Discipline

Discipline is the courage to hold onto the creative life force through a series of single moments strung together to complete a cycle of actions that reach a goal or outcome. Why do we tend to avoid self-discipline? Here are some reasons why we might come up against blocks in discipline:

- To avoid the responsibility of the moment;
- To avoid completing a creation;
- A fear of the wholeness or integrity of the moment;
- It forces us to be in the moment;
- It could mean change—playing a different game;
- It means slowing down and confronting yourself, your assumptions, and your beliefs about life, which might have changed.

I've often thought, as I'm sure you have also, that discipline is about physical suffering and conformity to the demands of an external person or thing like a boss or a schedule. I've come to understand that being in business is the discipline of controlling my own space through harnessing the power of a continuous string of single thoughts and applied actions to a single purpose that guides my days.

I've trained myself to think only positively even when confronted by no income three months straight and to act as though I do have a fledgling business by sitting down everyday and writing to the loyal readers of my e-newsletter. I've trained myself to integrate this business into my life as though I were adopting a child and, as such, giving it the *balanced* nutrition it needs—the necessary and appropriate attention, energy, and care.

There are days, like today, when I've dragged myself

out of bed at 10 a.m. (Scandalous!) I would peek at the fog in disgust from under my warm blankets *three times* before wrenching back the covers (still completely unwilling) to walk to my laptop and begin my day. I had no desire at all to do this on days like these—and with no good news on the horizon either. At least that's what my lousy mood told me to expect (it's a good thing I don't listen to my moods most of the time).

I have robbed myself of two hours of work this morning—the time I work best. I made the choice knowing I would have to put in the two hours later, perhaps on a Friday afternoon, when my daughter could be calling me about this or that and the phone could ring off the hook from her chattering teenage friends. So I'm working until 7 p.m. tonight. Today, I was completely undisciplined.

Discipline really comes down to the control of self—control of our personal environment made up of our many resources, including our continuous thoughts and actions. When we are growing a business organically through purpose and values, the pain doesn't put us off or make us procrastinate or sabotage our efforts; we revel in all that the journey brings. A rose, a potato, or a fir tree loves being exactly what it is; we too are here for a purpose and we must enjoy it.

Service

I waited anxiously in line like everyone else to have a *New York Times* best-selling author sign a book for me. The line advanced quickly, and when it was finally my turn, I handed her the book and watched in awe and disbelief as she barely looked at me, scrawled something illegible on the inside cover, then slid it across the table at me while giving the next person in line a glance as if to say, "Next!"

She had barely acknowledged my presence, barely said

thank you. What she did was squeeze out something that I could only guess was supposed to be a smile but what looked more to me like an unconscious twitch on the corner of her lip. Sure it was a book expo, and, yes, there were a lot of people lined up for her to sign, but forgive me if I'm wrong: isn't that a *good* thing?!

Although the books were free, this was a chance for her to personally connect with her readers—one of the few times an artist has a chance to control her environment. I saw no reason why this author wasn't bursting with enthusiasm to meet with her readership and to serve it in a more intimate way. After all, isn't that how you keep clients, readers, and customers? I asked myself: is service a dying art? Do people not know how to do it anymore? Do they simply not care? Was all this talk about great customer service being the cornerstone of business just talk?

The answers, at least in this situation, were irrelevant. And this afflicts more entrepreneurs than I care to admit. This author didn't believe, or couldn't see, that she was in business *and* that she was in business to serve. She thought she was just a writer and that was that. The truth is, we are never just painters, or just IT consultants, or just mothers or fathers, or just bookbinders. We're here to be of service to more than just ourselves, to improve the lives of others in any way we can, preferably with our skills and talents. The more people we can be of service to, the more money we make. It's that simple.

Luckily, my faith in entrepreneurs was to be redeemed because shortly thereafter, I picked up another book and headed over for the author to sign it for me. She was sitting by herself—no long lineups and no sullen looks, only a calm and serene air and smile greeted me as I sat down excitedly.

As I asked her to sign the book for me, I gushed, "I love your books and I can't wait to read this one. Can you sign it for me?" She smiled a bit and told me quite humbly that it wasn't her book, but she'd be happy to sign one of hers for me. I, of course, was mortified and I apologized.

We sat there a bit and talked about what the book was about and I left feeling richer somehow for knowing her, how she dealt with her situation at the expo, and that the storyline was awesome. She left me with more than an autographed book—she left me with an experience. That is the art of being of service. It is the willingness to enrich the life of someone with more than what they buy from you. Entrepreneurs have the gift of this service and it's one that can distinguish them from the ocean of imitations that litter the marketplace. Best of all, the art of great service doesn't cost a dime.

Freedom

Business is a journey into the soul to find freedom— freedom from our inner assumptions, pains, and demons. We can never consider ourselves free until our outer freedom mirrors what we are continually developing on the inside.

Outer and inner freedom is the opposite of slavery, whichever form it takes: your BlackBerry, your schedule, your many commitments and obligations, or your accomplishments. Enslavement is a habit that can be broken and transformed through conscious effort over time. If we are consciously engaged in our business, this liberation can and will happen. If after being in business we do not have the capacity to stretch *ourselves* to exhibit love, discipline, compassion, endurance, humility, communion, freedom, and leadership in every aspect of our lives, then we must ask what this journey of business has been for.

Freedom is a gift and sometimes it stretches us to the perceived limits of our character to use it wisely. This is what big business is facing right now. In order to be free, we must become masters of change—creative masters that find solutions to outdated, erroneous, ineffective systems or processes. It's a challenge that the organic entrepreneur takes as a way of life, not just as a business decision.

The overwhelming desire that we have as entrepreneurs to improve our situation is nothing but the desire for freedom—personal freedom on every level: financial freedom, freedom of choice, and freedom from our circumstances. But the freedom we get when liberated from our outer circumstances pales in comparison to the inner freedom that we will be challenged to find and maintain within ourselves if we allow ourselves to go deeper down the rabbit hole. Will you come?

Afterword

I wrote *The Organic Entrepreneur* to create a marriage between money and marketing, which I believe is the dynamic duo of *whealth*—a healthy relationship with money. I felt that money (the currency of capitalism that pervades our lives like no other tangible resource) and marketing (the way we make ourselves heard in a noisy world) are two of the most powerful yet misunderstood tools we use unconsciously everyday. Then I began asking, "Well, what if we added *consciousness* to the cocktail, what would we have then?" What could business become and how could it change the world if it were to be applied from the perspective of the transformed individual? Transformed by consciousness, transformed by love.

I wrote this book so that in each challenging moment of business, no matter what the season, you can look through the struggle and ask, "What is the season's inherent lesson?" The gifts of each season and the movement of awareness within each of these cycles remind us to *consciously* yield to something greater, to be silent and listen for our Greater Purpose to guide us in Winter. They remind us to *consciously* allow freer-flowing expression by removing any blocks to our energy systems in Spring, to *consciously* welcome abundance in our businesses through giving and gratitude and finally to accept the responsibility of economics and freedom through the *conscious* evolution of self-management with love, wisdom, and understanding.

I hope that this book will give these words—love, service, and consciousness—the freedom to reign within the structure and form of business and capitalism. It is a reminder to anyone, including myself, on those days that we forget that business is life and life is business—the free-flowing exchange of valuables for gain. These valuables can be anything, and the gain can be insight, tools, or coin. I wanted to write this book to draw the line in the sand, to give permission to include these words within the crucial conversations we have in business everyday when making deals, making money, or marketing our craft.

Each season, I am reminded to let go of what I think I know about business and begin each business transaction with love and ever-expanding consciousness—each new project, each new business partnership, each new product design. Use the gift of business as an opportunity to share with the world your unique talents to transform your life, the life of your business, and the lives of your customers. Since we cannot afford the price of ignorance and unconscious capitalism, I invite you to take these seasons and use them to cultivate your quest for gain with wisdom, love, and service, always in constant communion with your Source. If you've gotten this far, you're already on your way.

Index

abundance, 16-17, 28, 35, 37, 65, 123-126, 187
agreement, 106-108, 177
alignment, 25-27, 29, 108, 124
attraction, 100, 144, 168-169

beliefs, 15, 43, 51, 65, 85, 93, 106, 132, 134, 173, 175, 180
business, 13-17, 21-28, 30-35, 37-40, 42-68, 70-73, 77-93, 95-108, 110-113, 115-119, 123-126, 129-130, 132-144, 146-148, 152-155, 159-160, 165-176, 178-184, 187-188
map, 49-51, 60, 66
plan, 49, 52, 55, 56, 62, 104

capitalism, 121, 138, 187-188
currency of, 187
chaos, 26, 127, 129, 153
collaborating, 143, 145, 147-148
communication, 17, 28, 68, 93, 97, 123, 130-136, 147, 169
compassion, 71, 178-179, 183
compassionate capitalism, 138
connecting, 24, 143-145
reconnecting, 24, 33, 156

consciousness, 31, 56, 60, 93, 97-99, 107-108, 123, 130, 135-139, 165, 172, 187-188
conscious business, 98-99 102, 105, 136-138, 166, 170
conscious economics, 171
control, 42, 55, 59, 64-65, 69, 78, 90, 102, 119, 123, 153-155, 181-182
creation, 14, 16-17, 66, 72, 77-78, 98, 104, 106, 119, 180

discipline, 22, 65, 80, 180-181, 183

economy, 16-17, 106-107, 165, 172
economics, 166, 171, 187
entrepreneur, 13-17, 22-25, 27, 29-33, 35, 37-39, 41-43, 45-47, 49-51, 53, 55, 57-61, 63-67, 69, 71-73, 77, 79-81, 83-85, 87-91, 93, 95, 97-99, 101-103, 105, 107-113, 115-119, 125, 127, 129, 131, 133, 135-137, 139-147, 149, 151-155, 157, 159, 161, 167, 169-177, 179, 181-184, 187

failure, 64, 104-106, 142, 175
freedom, 33, 40, 147, 157, 166, 183-184, 187

giving, 15-16, 31, 123, 125, 141, 143, 152, 158-161, 187

goals, 43-44, 51, 65, 69, 71, 78, 80, 82, 85, 87, 90, 105, 109, 141, 147, 165, 168, 175, 180

gratitude, 28, 155, 157-159, 187

health, 15, 34, 38, 40, 54, 62, 94, 123, 137, 142, 154, 160, 167, 170-172, 175-178

incubation, 16-17, 19, 21

influence, 24, 30, 95, 102-103, 140, 144

integrity, 15, 26, 30, 45, 59, 93, 101-102, 106, 108, 180

investments,
  socially responsible, 160

listening, 15, 23, 24, 34, 67-70, 125, 131, 133-134, 154-155, 166, 170, 174, 177, 187

love, 17, 32-33, 37, 44, 47, 52, 64, 80, 84, 99-100, 109, 113, 116, 119, 125-126, 128-129, 131, 136, 139, 141, 144, 148, 151, 159, 168-169, 177, 182-183, 187-188

marketing, 14-15, 23, 33-34, 37-38, 46, 50, 52, 59, 80, 83, 85, 96-97, 99-100, 106, 108-114, 117, 126, 134, 174, 187-188

organic, 96-97

momentum, 59, 97, 119, 124, 139-141, 159

money, 15, 25, 31, 40, 43, 46, 55, 60, 64, 66-67, 69-70, 78, 81, 88-93, 95-96, 100-101, 106-108, 111-112, 116, 118-119, 126, 142, 157-158, 160, 167-168, 171-173, 182, 187-188

negotiating, 93-95, 133

patience, 17, 22, 24, 45-47, 52, 65-66, 77, 131

personal environment, 56, 130, 132, 144, 154, 166-168, 170, 172-173, 181

profit, 24, 32, 40, 46, 66, 73, 89, 91-92, 97-98, 113, 116, 126, 129, 138, 140, 170, 172, 179

purpose, 25, 30, 32, 34, 45-46, 50, 73, 89, 97, 123, 136, 138, 149, 171, 174, 177, 180-181
  Greater Purpose, 14, 24-30, 40, 49, 51, 59, 64-65, 78, 125, 138, 153, 173-174, 187

Research in Motion, 52

resonance, 168-169

respond-ability, 135

service, 25, 31, 83, 85, 110, 119, 133, 143, 155, 161, 169-170, 182-183, 187-188

soul, 13, 15, 30, 37, 39, 67, 89, 94, 98, 101, 116, 139, 144, 183
  see also spirit
spirit, 17, 31, 36, 40, 49, 66, 73, 97, 101, 115, 124, 129, 132, 138, 139, 156, 159, 161-160, 178
  see also soul
structure, 25, 33, 39, 49-50, 61, 85, 98, 110, 144, 160, 166, 188
S.W.O.T. analysis, 53-54

University of Waterloo, 52

values, 14-15, 30-32, 40-43, 45, 49, 51, 59, 61, 65, 94, 101-102, 106, 118, 124, 137, 149, 154, 159, 173, 178-179, 181
virtual assistant, 38, 146
vocation, 178

whealth, 40, 96, 187
winning, 22, 148, 152-153

vinegar + water - mirrors
to clean. c Slaves
simple black dress +
look-like the
real things plants
will carry the
milk grey.